POWER Over ALL

A 52-Week Guide to Victorious Living

AKILAH GRANT

POWER OVER ALL.

Copyright © 2012 by Akilah Grant.

All rights reserved. No other part of this book may be reproduced in any form or by any electronic or mechanical means including information storage and retrieval systems without prior permission in writing from the author; exceptions are made for brief quotations used in published reviews.

Cover Design: Shaw Concepts, Atlanta, Georgia, www.shawconcepts.com

Unless otherwise noted, all Scripture quotations are taken from the King James Version of the Bible.

All Scripture quotations marked (NLT®) are taken from the Holy Bible, New Living Translation®. Copyright © 1996, 2004, 2007 by Tyndale House Foundation. Used by permission of Tyndale House Publishers, Inc., Carol Stream, Illinois 60188. All rights reserved. All Scripture quotations marked (AMP) are taken from the Amplified® Bible. Copyright © 1954, 1958, 1962, 1964, 1965, 1987 by The Lockman Foundation. Used by permission. (www.Lockman.org)
All Scripture quotations marked (MSG or The Message) are from THE MESSAGE. Copyright © by Eugene H. Peterson 1993, 1994, 1995, 1996, 2000, 2001, 2002. Used by permission of NavPress Publishing Group.
All Scripture quotations marked (ERV) are from the Easy-to-Read™ Version. Copyright ©2006 World Bible Translation Center.

Definitions were compiled from the following:
Princeton University "About WordNet." WordNet. Princeton University. 2010. http://wordnet.princeton.edu
Public domain content from the 1828 Edition of the Webster's American Dictionary of the English Language. 2012. http://1828.mshaffer.com

Library of Congress Control Number: 2012922589

ISBN-10   0988510006
ISBN-13   978-0-9885100-0-5

Christian Life / Personal Growth / Inspirational

Printed in the United States of America.

Visit www.akilahgrant.com for more information.

*This book is dedicated to you.
Thank you for seeking the awesome power
God has placed inside of you.*

Presented To: Jennifer ~
Thank you for your wisdom and compassion in caring for our little ones. You truly have a precious gift. May the peace and power of God always be with you!
Sincerely,
A. Grant

From:

Date: Thursday, January 24, 2013

*In loving memory of my Grandma,
Marion Virginia Fisher Tyler.*

*Thank you for taking me to Sunday School
and for all the wisdom you shared
with me in your garden.*

༄༅

*This book is also dedicated to my husband,
Daires, with all of my love.*

*Thank you for your genuine support, kindness
and patience. Thank you for showing me that
there is no fear in love.*

*God is with us and He is for us!
- Romans 8:31*

Acknowledgements

*Thank you, Jesus and Holy Spirit, for guiding me.
Your love empowers me to overcome every life challenge.*

Thank you to all who purchase this book. I pray for abundance in your life, spirit and personal relationship with God.

*Thank you to my pastors and others who share the
Good News of Jesus Christ without compromise.*

Thanks to my editors who provided excellent input and to the most talented designer I have ever worked with. You all are an integral part of bringing this project to life.

*Thank you to my son, Daires Jr., and my little one on the way.
You are my reminder that God is a Creator and His blessings
are abundant and everlasting.*

Sincere thanks to my parents and family who always encourage me when I step out on faith.

A loving thanks to my little sister who impresses me with her unshakable faith and inner joy.

Thank you to my dear friends who hold me accountable, who motivate me and who are transparent with me. I love you all so much!

Thank you to those who provide me with unexpected opportunities to grow in God's love and ultimate power.

*I hope this book will be a source of power
and inspiration for you all!*

Table of Contents

Preface to POWER — 9

Your Guide to POWER — 12

FIRST QUARTER

Week 1: *First Priority, Final Authority* — 15
Week 2: *Believe* — 20
Week 3: *Love* — 26
Week 4: *You Are Anointed* — 33
Week 5: *Faith* — 38
Week 6: *The True Enemy* — 44
Week 7: *Sides* — 49
Week 8: *Learn to Fight* — 56
Week 9: *Prepare For Battle* — 61
Week 10: *Fearless* — 67
Week 11: *Your Army* — 73
Week 12: *Your Battle Cry* — 78
Week 13: *Encouragement* — 83

SECOND QUARTER

Week 14: *Power of the Tongue* — 87
Week 15: *Good Ground* — 93
Week 16: *Forgiveness* — 99
Week 17: *Healing* — 105

Week 18: *Grace and Glory*   111

Week 19: *Sow*   115

Week 20: *Never Outnumbered*   120

Week 21: *Peace*   125

Week 22: *Delivered from the Wicked*   130

Week 23: *Your Fortress*   136

Week 24: *Loyalty to God*   140

Week 25: *No Condemnation*   148

Week 26: *Look Ahead*   153

THIRD QUARTER

Week 27: *God's Word*   157

Week 28: *Pray and Give Thanks*   161

Week 29: *New Tongues*   167

Week 30: *Sound Mind*   173

Week 31: *All Things Work for Your Good*   178

Week 32: *Confidence*   183

Week 33: *Shine Your Light*   189

Week 34: *Think Big The Prayer of Jabez*   193

Week 35: *Leave Fools Alone*   199

Week 36: *Discipline Your Mind*   203

Week 37: *Guard Your Heart*   208

Week 38: *Haters*   212

Week 39: *Recover Quickly*   218

FOURTH QUARTER

Week 40: *Comfort and Strength*   222
Week 41: *You Are Chosen*   226
Week 42: *Believe God Is All*   230
Week 43: *You Are Blessed*   235
Week 44: *Consistency*   241
Week 45: *Free from Bondage*   246
Week 46: *Means of Escape*   251
Week 47: *Sweet Sleep*   257
Week 48: *Abound*   262
Week 49: *Truth*   266
Week 50: *Use Wisdom, Take Authority*   271
Week 51: *Good Success*   277
Week 52: *Victory!*   283

POWER Conclusion   287
About The Author   289

Preface to POWER

Power (noun): *force, energy; ability or strength; the faculty of doing or moving; that quality in any natural body which produces a change or makes an impression on another body*

Like many young people, I was ambitious and wanted to save the world. I thrived on being in the presence of those who made things happen and got things done. I was not interested in fame, but I definitely desired to have wealth, happiness, health and freedom. I wanted an abundance of goodness so I could share it with others. To accomplish my goals, I knew I needed extra power outside of myself.

When I began my quest in search of power, I did not have a personal relationship with God. Although I was saved, I did not even consider going to Him first. Instead, I researched popular books and products that were readily available to teach me how to take action over my life and become more powerful. What I found was that to control my own destiny, it requires a lot of strategic manipulation of people, words, and human interactions. Power from man-made methods put the burden of dominating people and circumstances all on me. This form of power was very dependent on my personal performance. I had to study and master power principles. I felt lost in the incessant responsibility of plotting and strategizing to create a better life. It was stressful to be in control all the time. As far as personal relationships, this power showed me how to attract a relationship, but not how to maintain one long term. It did not address the immense love and covenant required to maintain a peaceful home or how to overcome challenges with a spouse. The power strategies were great at attaining things in life, but not so much with preserving them.

With my attention on power from the world, I was not growing in the knowledge of God. I thought I was in control of my own destiny, but this self-created power wanted more and more from me as if I were in bondage to it. This power was like a hunger that could never be satisfied. If I did not do what it commanded at all times, I would not receive the reward. This power tried to crown itself as the divine ruler over my life. I did not want to become a megalomaniac. I began to question how this power could be sustained in my life when I made mistakes and grew weary at times. I realized this power was unable to protect me from myself.

Although frustrated, I knew there was a greater force of power somewhere, so I continued my quest. This time, it dawned on me to just go to the source and ask God. Almost overnight, my desire to understand His power consumed me. I had an urge to strengthen my personal relationship with Him and research the Bible. I saturated myself in the Word of God by listening to sermons, attending church regularly, studying and meditating on it. I began to pray more and ask for revelation. At first, it was extremely hard to let go of the control I thought I needed over my life. And besides, why would God do anything for me now? I had to be reminded that I was still His child whom He blessed. My greatest challenge was renewing my mind and yielding myself to Kingdom principles. Instead of always achieving, I had to begin receiving His love. I had to stop depending on my resources and start trusting His. While seeking God, I realized four important truths:

1. God loves me and His Spirit is within me
2. When I abide with God, He takes care of everything
3. God's power is everlasting and over all
4. As a Believer, I have unlimited access to His power

God answered all my questions with so much more insight than I ever envisioned. I discovered that the awesome power obtained through Him provides a peace beyond imagination because I do not have to create it. I have learned to depend on Him for everything, as well as, how to live and grow in His power.

That youthful desire to save the world never left. The Holy Spirit led me to write this book to spread the Good News of the Gospel to all who are willing to receive it. God shared with me that all who seek Him can experience His awesome love and power. Friend, know that He has a deep desire to show His power through you!

> *And they were astonished at his doctrine: for his word was with power.* **– Luke 4:32**

Your Guide to POWER

You believe what you say out of your own mouth more than you believe what anyone else says. This book provides weekly scriptures for you to meditate, confess and retain in your spirit. Meditation and confession are effective tools to increase your belief and faith in God. As your faith increases, His power intensifies within you.

Meditation is simply reflecting on what you read. Confession is speaking aloud through your mouth so that your own ears can hear what you say. It is vital for your spirit and flesh to hear you speak the Word of God over them. Once you have done this, you must acknowledge and believe His words by faith. Consistency in this process is sure to renew your spirit and transform your life. No matter where you are on your spiritual journey, this book will assist you in obtaining a richer understanding of God and His Word.

This book was created to be your guide to receive the power God has for you. However, you must believe in Him and receive the free gift of salvation through His Son, Jesus Christ in order to access this power.
If you would like to be born again in your spirit and accept Jesus Christ into your life, you can confess
*a **Prayer of Salvation**.*
One is provided for you in the Power Conclusion at the end of this book.

You may prefer to read one chapter each week to delve deeper into the topic before progressing. Or, you may want to read this book in its entirety and refer back to specific chapters as needed. Whichever method you choose, you will gain knowledge about God and His Word. You will also discover what you truly believe in your heart and how precious you are to Him. The Scriptures are taken from the King James translation of the Bible unless otherwise noted. You are encouraged to read other translations for better understanding of the Word. You can even record your personal journey and reflections in the companion *Power Over All: Journal Reflections and Bible Study Guide*. The main goal of this book is to be your inspiration and guide to God's power. Through this study of His Word, you will appreciate your connection to the amazing miracles, signs and wonders to come. At the end, you will be transformed and empowered to live everyday of your life - *victoriously!*

Meditate upon these things; give thyself wholly to them; that thy profiting may appear to all. – **1 Timothy 4:15**

Week 1:
First Priority, Final Authority

ಸಃಐ

Matthew 6:33
But seek ye first the kingdom of God,
and his righteousness; and all these things
shall be added unto you.

ಸಃಐ

Today is your day to get to know God more intimately instead of just knowing *about* Him. Seeking God and His kingdom must now be your number one priority. Family and work are important, but your personal relationship with God will prove to be the most vital to your future, your power and your well-being. God is not far away. When you accept Him, He dwells within your spirit. Your relationship with Him is the beginning to a renewed life better than you ever imagined. Seeking God, and His ways, brings everything you need and want freely to you. It is the *first* thing to do in every situation.

So what does it mean to seek?

Seek (verb): to go in search or quest of; to look for; to inquire for; to ask for; to solicit; go to or towards; to locate or discover

Seek requires action from you. It is a deliberate step towards God to find out about His ways. It is not just thinking about Him in your mind. Seeking is going after Him. Discover your Heavenly Father by reading His Word, praying and listening for His voice to speak to you. Set aside quality time each day to fellowship with Him. Open your heart and mind to new revelation as you search the Scriptures.

This week's Scripture will change your life forever. When you put God first, you have assurance that the Creator is taking care of everything on your behalf.

To put God first means that He is considered before anything else. In every situation, simple or complex, He takes first place before consulting any other source. If you are concerned about any area of your life - *health, relationships, marriage, finances, mental state, forgiveness, promotion, spiritual peace, your future* - seek God first. His restorative power will amaze you. At first, it will take a deliberate effort to always go to God first. But soon, your relationship with Him will develop to a point where you will naturally consult with the One who knows best. The opinions of others will not take precedence over what your Heavenly Father directs you to do. He must be your *final* authority in every situation.

When you seek God and His ways, you learn even more about yourself. You will be amazed at what your Heavenly Father already knows about you and what you did not know. This is just the beginning to becoming completely transparent with Him. He will show you the power that He has imparted within you. When you learn how God operates, you understand more about the world around you. He will give you answers to your questions and greater insight into the issues of life. This revelation knowledge does not come from one single prayer out of desperation. It comes from several conversations with your Heavenly Father. The more time you spend with Him, the more wisdom and confidence you obtain.

*And ye shall seek me, and find me, when ye shall search for me with all your heart.– **Jeremiah 29:13***

God says in His Word that He will add *"all these things"* to you when you seek Him first. Yes, everything you need and desire will be given to you when you make God first priority. Worry and uncertainty will no longer weigh you down or torment you. Worry is a main distraction from God and will keep you anxious, confused, hopeless and exhausted. Carrying the weight of your future on your own back can get overwhelming. Many people are depressed because they feel burdened by life. God wants to handle all things in your life so that you can focus on Him and your calling. Believing God and trusting Him to provide all your needs requires you to know Him personally, not just know of Him. You can see why seeking Him with all your heart must become first priority. Even if you have encountered times when circumstances distracted you from seeking Him, do not get caught up in punishing yourself. Start each day brand new with a desire to know more about God. He can restore time and He is always ready to spend it with you, day or night. Your entire quality of life and accessibility to power depends on your intimacy with God.

He wants a close relationship with you! Give it a try. Open the Bible and begin reading His Word for yourself. You will find out how the Kingdom of God operates. You will also be reminded of who and whose you are. Search for scriptures pertaining to your situation. You will be pleasantly surprised at how the Word of God speaks to you beyond the printed words on the page.

You will feel the power of God growing inside of you. Eventually, you will no longer be worried about what tomorrow may bring. A peace will come over you because you know He is taking care of everything. Your mind will fill with thoughts of your Heavenly Father and your spirit will be renewed. You will begin to act and react like Him. This is only the beginning! Before you realize it, your life will be completely transformed, simply because you chose to seek God and make Him first priority.

Make God your priority and begin to
establish your power!

Journal Reflections

Read Matthew Chapter 6 in its entirety.

How would you describe your relationship with God?

What is first priority in your life?

What or who are you spending your time with to learn more about?

How can you seek God more in your daily life?

How can you make God your final authority in all decisions?

Week 2: *Believe*

ಸಿಂಬ

John 12:44-46
*Jesus cried and said, He that believeth on me,
believeth not on me, but on him that sent me.
And he that seeth me seeth him that sent me.
I am come a light into the world,
that whosoever believeth on me
should not abide in darkness.*

ಸಿಂಬ

We live by our beliefs. Beliefs are powerful ideas in which our actions are based upon. They distinguish us from each other. Childhood beliefs are usually a combination of what we have experienced, what we have heard and what we have been exposed to. As we become an adult, we choose what we are now going to believe in, taking into consideration our current level of knowledge and understanding of the world around us.

Believe (verb): to expect or hope with confidence; to trust; to have a firm persuasion of anything; to accept as true

In this world there are many religious and spiritual beliefs. There are some who believe in God, and others who do not. Some believe in accessing the non-living for guidance; good spirits and evil ones. Some spiritual teachings want you to be self-lead with your mind instead of being led by God and His Holy Spirit. Our world holds such a broad spectrum of beliefs - higher-powers, inner-understandings, universal energies, mental explorations, conscious awareness, prophets, saints, sorcery, ancient wisdom, scientific theories and mysticism. No matter what the belief, they all seek to answer what is unclear to us. Mankind has always been curious about his origin, his purpose and his powers.

This week's Scripture is Jesus speaking and explaining that He is an extension of God with the purpose to deliver you out of darkness.

Your belief in God is a belief in Jesus and your belief in Jesus is a belief in God. When you read the Bible for yourself, you will know that God sent His Son Jesus to save you from sin and darkness. Jesus came to save you, not judge you. When you seek God, you will find answers to questions about your purpose and anything else you inquire. Some people have difficulty accepting Jesus as their Savior because they see Him separate from God. They do not believe Jesus is a requirement to have a relationship with God. However, if you choose not to believe Jesus, you reject God.

> *I and my Father are one.* – **John 10:30**

> *He that hateth me hateth my Father also.* – **John 15:23**

It can be confusing deciphering the different religious beliefs. Some beliefs take Jesus completely out of the equation, while others do not give him much significance at all. Some even convince people they must somehow pay for their sins, pay for their healing and pay for the blessing that Jesus already paid the price for. Sadly, there are beliefs that try to control others with man-made guidelines infused with words similar to God's Word. Others discredit the Bible as a mere book of fables or that the Old Testament is irrelevant to present day. All of this controversy can discourage a new, "baby" Christian or someone searching for the truth. One thing is for certain, the Word of God is clear and simple when you take the time to seek it for yourself. God speaks to you in the language and style you understand. Believe in Him and trust that He knows precisely how to explain even the most complex of theories.

> *But without faith it is impossible to please him:*
> *for he that cometh to God must believe that he is,*
> *and that he is a rewarder of them that diligently seek him.*
> *- Hebrews 11:6*

In my life, there was a defining moment the day I acted on my belief and accepted Jesus Christ as my Savior. Even though I grew up in church and always heard about God, I had not yet established a personal relationship with Him. I loved God in a childlike way, but did not really know the importance of Jesus in my life. One day, while I was a teenager, I was called to Him. I remember something inside of me nudging me after I heard the Word of God preached. It was not just about getting saved in order to go to Heaven. It was like there was an urgency and intense pull inside of my spirit to be closer with Him.

The day I got saved and accepted Jesus Christ as my personal Savior, I knew I had changed the course of my life. I felt a peace, love and acceptance never before experienced. At that time, I did not realize that accepting Jesus Christ was only the first step to an ever growing relationship. I thought it was the final act - now I am saved, so there is nothing else left to do. Unknowingly at the time, my choice to serve God made me a marked enemy to Satan and literally all "hell" broke loose.

I had no training on how to fight the dark ruler of this world or his demons. I faced an enemy I never confronted before. Due to my baby faith, ignorance and disbelief in certain areas of the Word, I encountered attacks that I did not have to suffer through. I thank God that He was patient with me and never left me, despite my shortcomings. It was vital for me to learn the ways of the Kingdom of God and to live in righteousness. Once I decided to seek Him for myself and read the Bible, I began to live and access the power of God that He already put inside of me. My firm belief in God, His Word and His Son, Jesus Christ, has given me power I never knew I had before. Friend, He put that same power inside of you!

As you continue to strengthen your belief and expand your knowledge of God, your power will increase. You will no longer live in darkness to your God-given talents and abilities. You will be able to do things that you never thought possible with the power of God.

Power to love
Power to forgive
Power to dominate
Power to heal
Power to think differently
Power to go forward
Power to overcome darkness
Power to increase
Power to transform lives
Power to live victoriously

Believe in God, His Son and His power!

Journal Reflections

Read John Chapter 12 in its entirety.

What do you believe regarding Jesus and His purpose in your life?

Why do you think people have had such a difficult time accepting Jesus?

What power do you need in your life?

What power did Jesus have through Almighty God?

What do you believe God can do for and through you?

Week 3: *Love*

༄༅

1 John 4:7
Beloved, let us love one another:
for love is of God;
and every one that loveth is born of God,
and knoweth God.

༄༅

This may shock you - ultimate power cannot function without love. God is love and God is power. Love is a very powerful force. Although the world may tell you love is weak, love is undeniably, one of the most important needs for mankind. Love can create and love can overcome all things.

You are God's beloved. He loves you more than any love you have ever experienced. He has loved you from the beginning of time - before you were created. He loves you even when you are not at your best. His love is everlasting. God wants you to know and understand His love so that you can share it with others. Knowing His love will bring you to a place of peace and power.

This week's Scripture instructs you to love others because God is love.

If you love God and know Him, you have love for everyone. He wants you to love those who may not love you in return, in addition to those who are not as easy to love. God wants you to love in the same way He loves. God wants you to love the lost and those in need of deliverance out of darkness. He wants you to love your neighbor. He wants you to love the goodness inside of you. He even wants you to love those who come against you.

God designed life to begin with the love between a man and a woman. Life is born, life grows, life shares and ultimately, life loves, multiplies and the cycle begins again. Life is ever living through love. Simple right? But somewhere along the way our world has tainted and complicated love. Love has been misrepresented by a lustful, emotional counterfeit that is unstable, shallow and fickle. This type of love does not endure. This love can be devastating and hurt others. Before gaining knowledge of God's Word, my definition of love was that it was the opposite of hate. I even believed love was the weaker of the two. I was so deceived and ignorant to God's love and its power.

Let us take a look at how the world generally describes love:

Love (verb): to be pleased with; to regard with affection; to get pleasure from

Love (noun): any object of warm affection or devotion; a strong positive emotion of regard and affection

While this counterfeit love sounds nice on the surface, it is missing a foundation. This love is dependent on feelings and emotions that are subject to change. This "fuzzy feeling" definition of love is incomplete. It is missing some of love's true characteristics as defined in the Bible.

Love is patient and kind.

Love is not jealous or boastful or proud or rude.

It does not demand its own way.

It is not irritable, and it keeps no record of being wronged.

It does not rejoice about injustice

but rejoices whenever the truth wins out.

Love never gives up, never loses faith, is always hopeful,

and endures through every circumstance.

- 1 Corinthians 13:4-7 (NLT)

God's love is sacrificial.

*For God so loved the world, that he gave his only begotten Son, that whosoever believeth in him should not perish, but have everlasting life. – **John 3:16***

God's love extends to those who do not deserve it.

*But I say unto you which hear, Love your enemies, do good to them which hate you, Bless them that curse you, and pray for them which despitefully use you. – **Luke 6:27-28***

Loving the way God loves is not easy. Fear, uncertainty, past hurt and bitterness can block the flow of love to you and through you. You need to know God and experience His love to even have the ability to love like Him. This requires such a trust in Him to lead and protect you when it comes to loving your enemies. He will guide you when it is time to love from afar. There are several examples of when God is the only one who knows how to handle delicate situations such as:

- an abusive parent or spouse
- an ungodly boss or co-worker
- a troubled child or sibling
- a deceitful friend or business partner
- a person who stole, betrayed or harmed you and your family in any way

If you stay focused on the love of God, He will take care of you and handle your enemies.

> *The LORD preserveth all them that love him:*
> *but all the wicked will he destroy.* **– Psalm 145:20**

Far too many people long for that "fuzzy feeling" love that was or is still missing in their lives. They look for love in all the wrong places. Because of this attachment to the counterfeit love, some find themselves in very dangerous and destructive relationships. This type of so-called love enslaves and does not *rejoice in the truth*. It has some of the same love talk, but it is controlling. This type of love is an imposter to God's love. It requires the recipient to prove his or her love through money, sex and never-ending deeds. This is not the love God has for you.

Scripture explains what love is not. Love *does not demand its own way* and love *is not irritable*. These are two characteristics that are very rare in today's society of selfish love. God's love *never gives up*. If only we all defined and practiced love the way Scripture does, we would set a new standard for the world!

Some people think that God does not love them. Horrible things done to them as a child, past mistakes or present misfortunes have caused them to harden their heart against Him. They do not realize that their bitterness towards God is exactly what Satan wants them to feel. Evil has impersonated love and given it a bad name. Evil "love" desires to entice, manipulate and betray leaving a person empty – or even worse - powerless. This imposter love comes in through empty and cracked spaces within the soul. Hurting people need to run to God and find out more about His love. This relationship with the Heavenly Father will provide insight essential to heal and recover from all pain. When you love God and the things of God, you are free. Pure love releases you from the chains of oppression that Satan tries to bind you with.

The good news is that when you have God's love inside of you, a protection comes with it. Blessing, joy, power and good success come with it, too. In essence, His love fills you and makes you whole. You no longer look to others to fill this void. There is no fear in God's love. You are made perfect through His love. It enables you to grow in love for yourself and others. As a result, you can give love freely and continue the cycle. You then begin to abound in love and experience the overflow in the lives of others. No matter how the world portrays love, your strength and power will increase as you share in the love of God.

> Know God more intimately and experience
> the most powerful force in the universe - love!

Journal Reflections

Read 1 John Chapter 4 in its entirety.

How would you describe your love for others? For God?

What prevents you from loving the way God loves?

How have you had to love your enemies?

Why is fear detrimental to love?

What can you do to increase in God's love?

Week 4: *You Are Anointed*

⚜

1 John 2:27
But the anointing which ye have received
of him abideth in you,
and ye need not that any man teach you:
but as the same anointing teacheth you of all things,
and is truth, and is no lie,
and even as it hath taught you,
ye shall abide in him.

⚜

In the fantasy or comic book realm, there is usually a natural man who obtains super-human powers to save the world. Depending on the story, these powers can come from a variety of sources - a far off galaxy, a scientific concoction, a bite from another species, a special piece of jewelry or from wearing a mask – just to name a few. In each case, the ordinary human is suddenly transformed into a superhero, possessing abilities far greater than the average man or woman.

Anoint (verb): to pour on; to smear or rub with oil

You can be transformed with supernatural power, too! As a Believer, your power source is the anointing of God through Jesus and the Holy Spirit. Once you received your salvation, the same power that Jesus received from God was poured on you and into your spirit through the Holy Spirit.

This week's Scripture tells you to remain in relationship with Jesus, who anointed you, and that this anointing will teach you everything you need or want to know.

The anointing of the Holy Spirit is truth, power and revelation. The anointing cannot come from mankind or any other source – only through God and His son, Jesus Christ.

> *Now he which stablisheth us with you in Christ, and hath anointed us, is God;* **- 2 Corinthians 1:21**

Why do I need God's power through the anointing of the Holy Spirit?

Here are just a few reasons why you need God's power of the anointing:

- to do God's good will on earth
- to accomplish your purpose in life
- to minister the good news of the Gospel
- to discern the truth
- to minister to and intercede for other Believers

- to live righteously in this world
- to be a stronger, more powerful Christian

Even Jesus needed this same anointing...

> *How God anointed Jesus of Nazareth with the Holy Ghost (Spirit) and with power: who went about doing good, and healing all that were oppressed of the devil; for God was with him. – **Acts 10:38***

What can the anointing do that I can't do on my own?

- demonstrate God's love and power
- heal and restore others
- destroy the yoke of Satan's oppression
- tread over all the power of the enemy
- open blind eyes and set people free
- strengthen and empower your spirit

*And it shall come to pass in that day, that his burden shall be taken away from off thy shoulder, and his yoke from off thy neck, and the yoke shall be destroyed because of the anointing. - **Isaiah 10:27***

*Behold, I give unto you power to tread on serpents and scorpion, and over all the power of the enemy: and nothing shall by any means hurt you. – **Luke 10:19***

How can I flow in the power of the anointing?

Just because you are equipped with the anointing, it does not mean you will automatically flow in it. As with many things of God, you must receive this precious gift in order to activate it. You may be wondering why you are not producing powerful, supernatural results in your life. There are a few things to note in order for the anointing to flow through you.

1. You must be willing to give up your life and live for God.

2. The anointing on you is for others. However, your life will reflect the presence of God's power.

3. You must be open to receive the flow of the anointing from other Believers.

4. The anointing is sacred.

You cannot grieve the Holy Spirit with jealousy, pride, unforgiveness, selfishness and other carnal emotions that block the flow of the anointing through you and to you. You must remain in relationship with Jesus Christ through prayer and righteous living. You do not have to be perfect – no one is. You simply honor and acknowledge God in all your ways. He cleanses you of your sins so that you can focus on your assignment. There is no special training required to flow in His anointing. He loves you and empowers you with everything you will ever need in this life. All you need to do is accept this precious gift and remain with Jesus.

Receive your supernatural power through
the anointing of the Holy Spirit.

Journal Reflections

Read 1 John Chapter 2 in its entirety.
How would you describe the anointing of God?
Describe a time when you helped others.
Were you flowing in the anointing?
Are you willing to work for God?
Do you believe the anointing of God is necessary to live a powerful life? Explain.
How can you remain in close relationship to Jesus to flow in the power of the anointing?

Week 5: *Faith*

෨෬

Matthew 17:20
And Jesus said unto them, Because of your unbelief: for verily I say unto you, If ye have faith as a grain of mustard seed, ye shall say unto this mountain, Remove hence to yonder place; and it shall remove; and nothing shall be impossible unto you.

෨෬

Have you ever believed something you have heard, although you have not yet seen it? Take for example a weather forecast. You may believe a forecast for the upcoming week and make outfit adjustments or travel plans based on the information. Why do you trust the forecast even though you have not yet experienced the future weather?

Maybe you or your spouse took a pregnancy test and it confirmed you were pregnant. What makes you believe the test without feeling or seeing the baby? There are certain things you trust to be predictors of future things to come even though you have not seen or experienced them yet. Faith is like your spiritual predictor, but on a much grander scale. Faith requires belief that anything is possible through God, including things that have not ever been done before. Faith is the *trust* and *belief* in what you hear in God's Word (the weather forecast or pregnancy test result) and knowing that it will come into existence in the future.

Let's look at two versions of the same biblical definition for faith:

> *Now faith is the substance of things hoped for,*
> *the evidence of things not seen.* **– Hebrews 11:1**

> *Now Faith is the assurance (the confirmation, the title deed) of the things [we] hope for, being the proof of things [we] do not see and the conviction of their reality [faith perceiving as real fact what is not revealed to the senses].* **– Hebrews 11:1 (AMP)**

Faith has also been described as an unstoppable, spiritual force that converts God's Word into power. Faith is a practical expression of your confidence in His Word. Faith is your greatest spiritual asset.

This week's scripture is Jesus' response to the disciples who asked why they could not cast the devil out of a young boy.

**He said if they had just a little faith,
nothing would be impossible for them.**

Jesus told the disciples that it was their unbelief and lack of faith that hindered them. If they would have had even a small amount of faith (the size of a grain of mustard seed), they could have cast out the devil, moved mountains and been able to do anything through God. Understand that great works cannot be accomplished through you if you have no faith in Him. Faith is mentioned numerous times throughout the Bible as the way of life for a Christian. Faith is mandatory to walk in God's power.

Most people have faith for what they believe can actually happen. Their faith often diminishes when it is time to believe what seems to be impossible - powers of darkness, complete healing from a terminal illness, restoration after devastation, or an abundant life with no formal education or training. Faith can be challenging because it requires consistency, endurance and absolute trust in God. It requires you to be unaffected by what you see, feel and hear in the present world, right now. You must exercise your faith daily. In the midst of life's tribulations, you have to believe that the future will be how God says it will be...fruitful, abundant, peaceful, victorious and full of joy.

Maybe you have faith, but it is strong in only one area, similar to my situation. Although I had strong faith in healing, I had little faith in speaking things that are not as though they were.

For example, if anything tried to come against my body, without a doubt, I believed I was already healed according to the Word of God. My actions and words aligned with the Scriptures of health and long life. No matter what I felt like, I did not let my current health condition steal my joy or confidence in God. My faith in healing worked every time. But in other aspects of my life, my mouth was too busy speaking the current situation. In areas such as finances, relationships, work and every day needs; I had little faith. It was little because it was not big enough to endure or last long enough to see any manifestation. My faith was muffled by skepticism and worry. I only communicated what my senses could detect: fear, lack, discomfort, strife, etc. My words and my heart were in total opposition to faith in those areas other than healing. I was more like a news reporter re-capping the major headlines of disaster instead of a faith forecaster predicting a positive outlook for the future. I realized that in order to be powerful, faith must be big in every area of life!

So how can you increase in faith?

Reading and hearing the Word of God is always a good start to anything, especially faith building. Next, you practice speaking words that align with God's Words. One of my favorite Scriptures to meditate on and confess for faith building is:

> *I can do all things through Christ
> which strengtheneth me. – **Philippians 4:13***

It is so simple, yet packed with faith and power! In one week of meditating the Word of God in a specific area, you will be able to tell a difference. Your trust in God and understanding of the Word will increase. Over time, your confidence to believe what you say is established and your faith is enlarged. Now, you can begin to work your faith by believing God for something you cannot handle in the natural. It means to do what the Word of God says, not just to hear or recite His words. It is important to exercise your faith so it can become stronger and you learn how not to be moved or deterred by emotions or circumstances.

Standing in faith until what you believe is manifested is a true test of your trust in God. During these times it is vital to remain focused on Him and not to waiver. Be sure your belief is aligned with the Word of God regarding your situation. Seek Him for clarity if what you believe has not yet manifested. Faith reveals areas of doubt and uncovers true beliefs. You should engage with people of strong faith, who think big and who love God. Beware of being in the presence of and listening to faith doubters. They use intellect, science, reasoning or even your past to convince you that your faith is not realistic and that what you believe will not come to pass. Most often they have good intentions and want to provide you with practical options other than faith. However, faith doubters will believe a medical prognosis, an economic report, a political opinion, or news broadcast before they believe the

Word of God. For this reason, doubters can be detrimental to you during a crucial time of standing in faith.

That your faith should not stand in the wisdom of men, but in the power of God. – **1 Corinthians 2:5**

Instead, surround yourself with faith warriors who can testify to the greatness and glory of God! Your faith will continue to strengthen and enlarge. Faith to overcome anything is necessary to please God and live victoriously.

Build your faith, build your power!

Journal Reflections
Read Matthew Chapter 17 in its entirety.
Describe a situation where your faith was strong.
Which area(s) of life do you have doubts about God's power?
(health, finances, deliverance, forgiveness, relationships, etc.) Why?
What Scriptures can help you increase your faith
in those areas?
What encourages you and builds up your faith?
What can you do daily to exercise your faith?

Week 6: *The True Enemy*

෨෬

Ephesians 6:12
*For we wrestle not against flesh and blood,
but against principalities, against powers,
against the rulers of the darkness of this world,
against spiritual wickedness in high places.*

෨෬

People are not the enemy. The real enemy is Satan and his demons. He is the most deceitful, wicked opponent you will ever face. His centuries of lying, stealing, accusing, killing, destroying and deceiving far surpass any human knowledge. You are not equipped to fight him with your own strength. Most importantly, Satan is not as powerful as God.

This week's Scripture explains that your enemy is not the human flesh and blood that you see in the natural, but it is the dark powers and spiritual wickedness.

Your enemy is spiritual wickedness in high places. Initially, this truth can be a bit overwhelming since you live in a physical world. You usually see the people who cause you pain before you realize the spirit working through them. However, a person is not the enemy. Do not assign a face to the opponent. Not physically reacting to a person hurting you can be very hard to do. More so, the thought of spiritual warfare, fighting principalities and rulers of darkness can be a bit daunting. Thankfully, God is always with you and will lead you to victory in every situation.

Satan is described as using three main weapons:

Satan uses **deception:**

Deceive (verb): to ensnare; be false to; be dishonest with; cause someone to believe an untruth or disbelieve what is true

Deception (noun): that which deceives; a misleading falsehood

Satan uses **temptation:**

Tempt (verb): to incite or solicit to an evil act; to try; to prove; to provoke someone to do something through (often false or exaggerated) promises or persuasion

Temptation (noun): something that has the quality to seduce; solicitation of the passions; enticements to evil proceeding from the prospect of pleasure or advantage

Satan uses **accusations:**

Accuse (verb): To charge with a fault; to blame; to charge with an offense against the laws

Accusation (noun): the act of imputing blame or guilt; the charge of an offense or crime

Satan uses these weapons with the sole purpose of distracting you away from God. Your physical senses: hearing, feeling, smelling, tasting and seeing can be easily beguiled. These natural senses are the only realm Satan can operate in. He uses people and circumstances to affect your physical senses and negatively influence your thinking. Satan often uses words that you hear through television and other people to confuse, frustrate, and oppress you. He wants you to doubt the Word of God, so he attacks your self-identity and self-worth. You have to make sure you know who you are and whose you are - a precious child of God!

Deception is used to make you believe something that is false. It is also the act of hiding or blinding the truth to make you *not believe* what is true. This is called doubt. Deception is often the hardest enemy to detect. You may battle with not believing the truth in the Word of God because you have not read the Word for yourself to find out what it actually reveals. Another reason may be because you did not realize that Satan uses people and circumstances to keep you questioning the true power in God's Word alone. Doubt is a very subtle weapon. More so, doubt is extremely devastating to your faith.

And he that doubteth is damned if he eat, because he eateth not of faith: for whatsoever is not of faith is sin.
- *Romans 14:23*

Satan uses fear and doubt to control you. One of the biggest deceptions that Satan uses is to convince you to doubt God's love for you. Satan tries to make you feel unworthy through accusations and by bringing up past mistakes over and over again. Many people still battle with "low Christian identity," as I once did. They think they must suffer financially, physically or even mentally because doubt enters into their mind to make them feel unworthy of God's blessing. Reading His Word is the only thing that reveals the truth about you as His precious child. Satan does not want you to be assured that you are with God and that He is with you. He wants you to feel disconnected to your Heavenly Father. Once Satan weakens your faith and gets you to think you are alone, he attacks. His mission is to steal, kill and destroy – steal your joy, destroy your life and kill your spirit. Satan will use any person or situation against you.

The lie that says God does not love you with your human faults or that He is upset with you is an old tactic. Unfortunately, it still works with people today. Without revelation of God's love and power, they live a defeated life. The truth is, God ALWAYS loves you. Yes, He loves you even when you make mistakes that cause shame. Repent and move forward with Him. Many times, God gets the blame for tragedy and hardships that He did not send, while Satan sits back and watches your heart harden against the only One who can deliver and restore you. Satan uses your emotions to fluster you. During these times it is important to run to God and seek wisdom for revelation of truth in that particular situation. When you fellowship with Him, you will find the solution to overcome all.

Remember, the true enemy is Satan and he will use temptation, shame, guilt, lies, tragedy and anything else to cause you to disconnect yourself with God. From now on, you will no longer fall into that snare. God loves you at all times and under any circumstances. Fortify yourself daily with the truth of His Word. Your power through God is no match for spiritual wickedness.

Stay connected to God for power over the true enemy!

Journal Reflections
Read Ephesians Chapter 6 in its entirety.
Describe a time when you may have been deceived, tempted or accused by Satan.
Describe your spiritual identity in God.
How do you deal with the actions or words of other people that try to disconnect you from God?
What is something new you can incorporate to stay connected to God?

Week 7: *Sides*

ಸಿಂಡ

Matthew 6:24
No man can serve two masters:
for either he will hate the one, and love the other;
or else he will hold to the one, and despise the other.
Ye cannot serve God and mammon.

ಸಿಂಡ

This world gives us many options and opinions. It takes polls and shares results to see how many people agree with a certain viewpoint. Whatever is popular and gets a majority of support is usually what is promoted via talk shows, internet, radio and other media. Some people are swayed into changing their mind when they find out how many people agree with the other side. Their standard is not based on the Word of God, but on the world's opinion of what is "normal" or "correct." The danger in the world's standard is that it is unstable and ever changing. However, God's standard never changes. You can be assured that your Heavenly Father will always remain the same.

> *Serve (verb):* to work for; to bestow the labor of body and mind in the employment of another; to attend to command; to submit to; to obey and worship

> *Mammon (noun):* a personification of wealth and avarice as an evil spirit

This week's Scripture is a warning that you cannot serve and obey two masters.

Figuratively speaking, what side of the fence are you on? Those who believe they are on neither side are, by default, on Satan's side. There is no "neutral" ground when it comes to God or Satan. You cannot straddle the fence, nor can you keep switching your location. You may desire to be on God's side but cannot let go of this world's system or lifestyle. Be certain from which side you are actually being lead and taking advice. Take notice on which side you are living. Your happiness and peace are directly connected to whatever side you choose.

If you try to serve both God and evil, you will only love one. You will hate, despise and resent the other. This Scripture is telling you that it is not possible to serve both. Your loyalty and power will lie with the one you love. So why is the decision of who you serve so important? Your quality of life and your depth of power depend on the master you choose to serve.

Unfortunately, most of the present day sociological norms regarding family, finance and personal conduct oppose the kingdom of God and righteous living. God's ways are becoming more unpopular and evil is spreading its influence into the world. You do not have to yield to the pressure of agreeing with worldly doctrine. You must remember that you always have the option to choose. God wants you to choose life with Him.

> *Love not the world,*
> *neither the things that are in the world.*
> *If any man love the world, the love of the Father is not in him.*
> *– 1 John 2:15*

Issues in your life can get very complicated, especially when you try to deal with them under two masters. A little bit of world knowledge mixed with a little bit of God's knowledge is dangerous. Jumbling principles can leave you powerless over a situation. God's side has a different standard than the world. Here are examples of life topics that continue to cause controversy and confusion in those that have not chosen a side:

The World's Changing Opinions vs. **God's Unchanging Word**

Money Management

Borrow to get what you want

Owe no man - Lend, sow and tithe

Health

There is no cure for some diseases
You are healed through the blood of Jesus

Marriage

Not worth it - Just live together
Whoever makes the most money runs the household
Divorce if you can no longer get along
A man and a woman cleave together and submit to one another as onto God - Man is the head
Marriage is a forever covenant

Sex

Acceptable between two or more consenting adults
Created to be between a man and a woman after marriage to bond and reproduce

People Who Have Hurt You

Never forgive and get revenge – Curse them
Forgive and let God have His vengeance – Bless them

Life Advice

Live for the moment - Live in the now
You can help yourself without God
Live by faith - Be blessed to be a blessing
You need the Savior, Jesus Christ, to redeem you

Children
They are expensive
Do not ever spank your children - Do not pray in school
They are a blessing
Discipline your children in love - Do not spare the rod
Train up a child in the way he or she should go

Purpose
Do whatever makes you feel good
Use your God-given talents to spread the Good News of the Gospel and bring others into their salvation

Creation
Science and man created everything in the galaxy today
God is the creator of all: heaven, earth, atoms, life, etc.

For all that is in the world, the lust of the flesh,
and the lust of the eyes, and the pride of life, is not of the Father,
but is of the world. – 1 John 2:16

Far too many times I care to admit, I struggled with playing the fence. One moment I was playing by the world's rules and the next moment, I was living by God's precepts. Even worse, there were times when I did not live by any set standards except the ones I justified in my head. I was like those who did not claim to be on either side. I compromised my finances, my body, my heart and my time, just to fit in with other un-sided people.

I was once referred to as the *cool Christian*. I was living as a worldly person professing to love God. I was ignorant and selfish. I even explored other "spiritual" beliefs that were associated with powerful and successful people that I admired at the time. But I always had one issue that kept me from converting over - I believed in Jesus Christ as the Son of God and my personal Savior. Dwelling in the "grey" area, I thought I was living neutral and would not upset anything or anyone. But spiritually, I was an enemy to God from the other side. Trying to live "sideless" made me powerless, useless and frustrated. During that time in my life, I was not a living example of the power of God.

Ye cannot drink the cup of the Lord, and the cup of devils:
ye cannot be partakers of the Lord's table, and of the table of devils.
- 1 Corinthians 10:21

Choosing a side does not mean you look down on others who are not on your side. It simply means you have decided how *you* are going to live and who *you* are going to serve no matter what the situation. If you choose God's side, you will have a greater love and compassion for those unaware that they could be serving two masters. If others see you living a healthy, victorious life, they will want to know more about the God you serve. People are attracted to power and its source.

In every area of your life, you will be confronted with the decision to choose a side. This will be a consistent, daily process until you are rooted and grounded in righteousness. Unnecessary and unpleasant events can occur in life when you are "lukewarm" about choosing God's side. When you anchor yourself in Kingdom principles, you close the gate to the evil side and it no longer has direct access to you. Some days, you may find yourself drifting too close to the fence. No worries - continue to abide with God more and more each day. As you gain understanding, it becomes a joy to live with Him and to serve Him.

Serve on God's side and remain there!

Journal Reflections
Re-read Matthew Chapter 6 in a different translation other than the King James Bible.
What side of the fence does your life reflect? Explain.
What challenges do you feel you would encounter living solely on God's side?
What changes do you need to make to ensure your life reflects God's way?

Week 8: *Learn to Fight*

ಸಧಿಲ

1 Timothy 6:12
*Fight the good fight of faith,
lay hold on eternal life, whereunto thou art also called,
and hast professed a good profession
before many witnesses.*

ಸಧಿಲ

Spiritual warfare demands a new set of fighting skills. Whether you like to fight or have never fought before, your first spiritual training will be to learn how to *fight the good fight of faith*. It is quite different than natural fighting, because with faith, you win every time. If you have fought before, you can appreciate a victorious outcome before you begin. Remember, your battle is not against flesh and blood. No matter if you are an amateur or a professional, you can sharpen your skills and learn how to fight the good fight of faith.

Fight (noun): to strive or contend for victory, in battle or in single combat; a hostile meeting of opposing forces

This week's Scripture is a directive to seize the eternal life God has given to you who are saved and to fight the good fight of faith.

So what does it mean to fight a good fight of faith?

Well, let's focus on the "good fight" part. A good fight means that you win no matter what the circumstances. Not only do you win, but you get to enjoy the victory without battle scars afterwards. You win against an evil enemy without injuries to innocent bystanders. Now that is a *good* fight!

In this type of combat, you encounter oppositions to your faith. The battleground is anywhere you see, feel, hear, think and experience things with your flesh (body) or natural senses that do not align with the Word of God. You fight against negative past experiences that try to establish strongholds in your life. You fight against lack, depression, sickness, fear, low self-esteem, oppression, addiction, stress and other tools of the enemy. Your fight is to keep your faith strong and focused on God during these times of adversity.

The good fight of faith is a real fight and one you may need to fight daily. At first, it can seem distressing to fortify your faith in the midst of tragedy or loss. It can seem impossible when you receive a bad report, discover betrayal, or when you encounter your darkest hour. This world never ceases to promote a sense of fear, a feeling of oppression, low self-worth and a message of lack. Fighting for your faith never ends.

So how can you build up your faith?

So then faith cometh by hearing, and hearing by the Word of God – **Romans 10:17**

Faith comes by hearing the Word of God. You have to continue reading the Word, hearing the Word and confessing the Word to yourself. Once an attack comes that tries to make you counteract in the flesh, put on your shield of faith. All of the Word that you have heard and meditated on becomes your protection. Whatever it is that is coming against you will not be able to penetrate through your faith. The Word of God provides wisdom, strategy and insight concerning the victory you already have over every situation. Now, your faith is impervious to the everyday challenges of life. Your faith fighting skills are strengthened with each battle.

I once received a medical report that told me I had a disease. I was devastated on impact from the negative words that came out of the nurse's mouth. I immediately cried and felt defeated. I even confessed the bad report to my family and a close friend. After a few hours of dwelling in one of the darkest valleys I have ever encountered, my spirit reminded me to fight for my faith. I had to make a decision…do I accept defeat or do I fight the *good* fight. I chose to fight.

My faith, based on God's promise of health, was in complete opposition to what the medical tests reported. It was a fact that the tests showed a disease, but the truth was that I was already healed and healthy beyond measure. Despite how I felt, I began meditating on my healing scriptures and confessed I was healed. I told my body that it did not have to accept this disease and that no disease has permission to dwell in it. I repented for speaking negative words in agreement with the bad report. Over the course of a few days, a peace came over me. I believed and confessed my healing scriptures in faith diligently day and night. I did not speak about the disease any more. After about a year from that time, I had to take another test and no disease was found in my body. Instead of trying to fight the disease solely in the natural; I decided to fight to keep my faith in healing strong. In the end, I won! Faith is the most powerful force to winning every time!

You will always have a choice, whether to fight the good fight of faith or to accept something that is not of God. Satan will always attempt to wreak havoc in your life by presenting challenges, but he cannot win against you when you are protected by the full armor of God and your shield of faith. Do not confuse faith fighting with trying to fight someone else's battle. You are not directly absorbing the attacks of the enemy so it is easier for you to be strong over their situation. Stay focused on building your faith for what God is doing in your life. It is imperative that you learn to fight the good fight for yourself. While you are in the midst of feeling the pain or discomfort, your faith must activate and remain consistent. This is a much harder encounter than having faith for someone else. It is the true fight of faith. Your confidence and testimony of victory will encourage others to fight their good fight of faith. The enemy is relentless; therefore, your faith must be unyielding. Remember that in a good fight, you always win. Fighting the good fight of faith is essential to growing in God's power.

Learn to fight with the power of faith!

Journal Reflections
Read 1 Timothy Chapter 6 in its entirety.
How would you describe a good fight?
What hinders your faith?
Describe the power of faith in your own words.
How can you increase in hearing the Word of God and strengthen your faith?
Describe what a victorious life looks like to you.
What area(s) in your life do you need to begin fighting with faith?

Week 9: *Prepare For Battle*

ঝওত্ত

Ephesians 6:10-11
*Finally, my brethren, be strong in the Lord,
and in the power of his might.
Put on the whole armour of God,
that ye may be able to stand against
the wiles of the devil.*

ঝওত্ত

There will be battles ahead so now is the time to prepare. Satan is not going to leave you alone without testing your faith or defying your power. He will come at you from every side and at every level. Have no fear; God gave you His armor so that you can stand against every trick of the devil.

This week's Scripture commands you to be strong in God and His mighty power by putting on His whole armor.

Do not depend on your own ability. You will only be able to protect yourself from the tricks of the devil when you put on the whole armor of God. This armor is more than just a physical protection; it protects your spirit and soul. It is more durable than a knight's suit of armor and more advanced than any soldier's combat gear. It is made from the spiritual attributes of God: **truth, righteousness, peace, faith, salvation and Holy Spirit.**

Let's take a closer look at each piece of armor.

Stand therefore, having your loins girt about with truth, and having on the breastplate of righteousness; **- Ephesians 6:14**

Truth (noun): veracity; purity from falsehood; exactness

Truth cleanses and sets people free. Some try to suppress it, but truth does not waiver or change over time. Truth brings light to a situation even if you are unable to handle its brightness. Truth is not always found in facts. It is very powerful and must be respected. We will explore truth in depth in a later chapter.

Loin (noun): the space on each side of the vertebrae, between the lowest of the false ribs and the upper portion of the haunch bone; the core of generative power

God wants you to wrap truth around your body where life-giving power and your core strength abide. Everything you produce must be of life-giving truth.

Righteousness (noun): adhering to moral principles; purity of heart and rectitude of life; conformity of heart and life to the divine law; the perfection or holiness of God's nature

Righteousness requires you to judge your own actions, judge your own heart and act in accordance to God's Word. He wants you to protect your heart with virtue and honor. You will need your breastplate of righteousness when you stand against an unscrupulous, immoral demon spirit. You put on these pieces of armor when you operate as a person of integrity and good character.

And your feet shod with the preparation of the Gospel of peace; **- Ephesians 6:15**

Peace *(noun): a state of quiet or tranquility; freedom from disturbance or agitation, fear, terror, anger, anxiety or the like; calmness; quiet of conscience*

Peace is something that dwells inside of your spirit. Peace does not come from others and cannot be taken by others. God wants your feet covered and prepared with peace – free from fear. Even though you are in warfare, you are to be composed with your feet standing firm against the enemy. There should be an inner calmness that you possess in the midst of a storm. His peace gives you assurance. You put on this armor by believing and being grounded in the Gospel of Jesus Christ. This requires a personal relationship with your Heavenly Father.

> *Above all, taking the shield of faith, wherewith ye shall be able to quench all the fiery darts of the wicked.*
> *– Ephesians 6:16*

> ***Faith*** *(noun): an affectionate practical confidence in the testimony of God; to believe; to obey*

Faith allows you to know, obtain and receive things in your spirit before it appears in the natural world. Faith protects you from what the enemy puts in front of your eyes to distract, deceive and keep you in bondage to the flesh and your emotions. Faith usually disagrees with your physical senses, but it gives you a spiritual perspective in all situations. God wants you to have your shield of faith ready to extinguish all of the fiery darts of doubt that Satan will bombard you with. You carry this important piece of armor by staying focused on His Word.

> *And take the helmet of salvation, and the sword of the Spirit, which is the word of God:* **- Ephesians 6:17**

> ***Salvation*** *(noun): the redemption of man from the bondage of sin and liability to eternal death, and the conferring on him everlasting happiness; deliverance from enemies; victory*

Salvation is a free gift from God to all who choose it. You are delivered from sin and able to receive His joy. He wants your helmet of salvation to guard your mind against temptation, condemnation and sin consciousness. These are all thoughts and emotions that the enemy will use against you. Your helmet is a vital piece of spiritual armor that should be worn at all times.

Spirit, in this verse (Ephesians 6:17), is defined as the Word of God. He wants you to use His words to advance towards His promises and defend yourself by cutting down the enemy. Satan cannot prevail over God's Words. When you only say what God says, your power is ignited. There is no need to add any words of your own. Adding words will dilute or even cancel your power. Jesus used the Word of God only against Satan and defeated him.

And Jesus answered and said unto him, Get thee behind me, Satan: for it is written, Thou shalt worship the Lord thy God, and him only shalt thou serve. – **Luke 4:8**

Not only will your sword of the Word penetrate the enemy, it will nourish your spirit, strengthen it, and fortify you during your time of conquering the enemy. You put on these pieces of armor by knowing your Kingdom rights and privileges as a child of God.

Spiritual warfare is real. Acquiring each attribute of the armor of God will lead you to victory all the days of your life. The evil in this world is always orchestrating new situations through economic turmoil, family issues, world tragedy, relationships, sickness, business, etc., to deceive you and weaken your faith. Not only must you defend your faith, but there may be a time when you must be ready to initiate an attack against wickedness. You will need the whole armor of

God, not just one piece. Always remember, no demonic force is greater than you when you fight together with God. He provides you with the armor, but you must put it on.

Meditating on this Scripture can also bring an assurance of His power over any circumstance. Everything you will ever need comes through the Word of God directly into your spirit. Your born again spirit always operates in Godly wisdom. When you protect yourself with His armor, you can go forward in confidence of victory.

Be bold in God's power by putting on
His whole armor!

Journal Reflections
Re-read Ephesians Chapter 6 in a different translation
other than the King James Bible.
Which piece of armor are you most comfortable with wearing
and is the most effective for you? Why?
Which one is difficult for you to wear? Explain.
What area(s) of your life do you need to put on
God's whole armor?
How can you grow stronger in each spiritual attribute
of God's armor?

Week 10: *Fearless*

※

Isaiah 35:4
*Say to them that are of a fearful heart,
Be strong, fear not: behold,
your God will come with vengeance,
even God with a recompense;
he will come and save you.*

※

Most of us have feared something at least once in our lives. Fear can cripple and debilitate even the strongest person. It brings worry, frustration and poor decisions. In the world we live in, fear is often used to control and influence us into a specific thought or action. The world perpetuates the fear of "running out" - running out of water, food, jobs, money, time, clean air, trees, animals, medicine, gas and resources, etc.

Satan feeds into the fear of lack, the fear of loneliness and the fear that no one can save you. Sometimes fear hides deep inside of you. It is a negative emotion, whether real or imagined that hinders progress and undermines your power with God.

Maybe you have heard the definition of fear as *false evidence appearing real*. You sometimes fear things that are not even real. You may have feared "the boogie man" when you were little, but as you got older; you realized he does not exist. As you experienced life, you may have feared rejection, making a mistake or a negative outcome. Although these things may not have turned into reality, fear caused you to react as if they will or already have.

Fear (noun): a painful emotion or passion excited by an expectation of evil, or the apprehension of impending danger; anxiety; dread; terror

Vengeance (noun): infliction of pain on another, in return for an injury or offense; retribution; revenge

Recompense (verb): to compensate; to make return of an equivalent for anything given, done or suffered; to return an equivalent; to repay

This week's Scripture tells you not to fear, but to be strong in the Lord because He will save you.

Do not fear anything. God will save you, He will punish your enemies, and He will compensate you for everything you have lost. God does not believe that a little fear is good for you so that you can become courageous. No, He wants you to be fearless. It takes courage to relinquish fear and go forward in life. This requires complete trust, boldness and confidence in your relationship with Him.

A little fear brings a little doubt. As mentioned earlier, doubt is an opposing force to faith. Fear is a burden and a hindrance to good decision making that blinds you from the truth. Fear does not lead you to a desired destination. It leads to a path of self-destruction, depression and desolation. That is exactly where the enemy wants you to be. You do not have to worry or take matters into your own hands. God does not leave you abandoned. He wants you to be fearless so you can live a full and prosperous life. God will unleash His power to restore you and to inflict revenge on your adversaries.

There is a story of a young lady who grew up very poor. Her family lived among others who were struggling, but they were the type of poor that experienced no food, no heat, nothing new and no joyous holidays. She and her family suffered while the world around them seemed to delight in fun times together. Despite her hard upbringing, she blossomed into a beautiful, intelligent, hard-working lady with a lovely personality. She worked her way through college and was able to obtain a great job with all the perks. Most would consider her to be financially stable and a very good catch.

While attending a business conference, she met a responsible, loving man with a good job. Soon, they were married and living quite well. However, as they built their life together, they always had financial issues - in her eyes. It was not that they had money management problems; they both were very savvy with finances. The issue was that they could not save enough to make her feel secure. Unfortunately, her husband got laid off from his job and they had to use their savings to continue their current lifestyle. Each time she and her husband dipped into their savings, memories of being without tormented her. Although they had plenty in savings to cover their costs and he was able to find a new job within six months, her immense fear of lack consumed her. Hastily, she divorced her husband and went back to school to obtain another degree. She was convinced that her decision to get another degree and get rid of an extra mouth was her only option to prevent poverty. Satan continued to remind her of the pain and shame of poverty and lack. Regardless of her financial status, it was never enough to overcome the fear. Satan was out to steal her peace, her marriage and ultimately, her connection with God. Her fear was stronger than her faith and so she carried the weight of provision all by herself.

Having experienced poverty in her childhood, the deep fear of not having enough amplified to an extreme level when she became an adult. It was not revealed until she had to work together with her husband. Had she discovered the power of God within herself; she would have remained in her marriage and allowed Him to deliver her from the fear of lack. She would have experienced His restorative and healing power. Childhood experiences can often plant deep-rooted fears that create bitterness towards God as an adult. Satan will magnify and use these fears against you. In these situations, it is vital to open your heart to God to gain understanding and clarity about what was happening in the spiritual realm while you were a child.

When you operate in fear, you block yourself from God's ability to save you. Power cannot co-exist with fear. Throughout the Word of God, it repeatedly tells you to *fear not*. You are not to fear any enemy, whether real or perceived. Look at what Moses said to the children of Israel when they feared the attack of Pharaoh and his mighty army...

And Moses said unto the people, Fear ye not, stand still, and see the salvation of the LORD, which he will shew to you to day: for the Egyptians whom ye have seen to day, ye shall see them again no more for ever. The LORD shall fight for you, and ye shall hold your peace. - **Exodus 14:13-14**

In any biblical translation of this scripture, it is clear that God does not want you to fear. He wants you to be at peace. He wants to ensure you that He will destroy your enemies for you. Better yet, you will never have to see them again when you overcome your fear. He will restore all that is lost. No one can do all of that for you, except God who *is* love. Allow Him into your heart and be fearless!

Take inventory of any fears that expire today!

Journal Reflections

Read Isaiah Chapter 35 in its entirety.

What has been your biggest fear(s)?

What makes you feel safe and secure?

Why does God want you to not fear anything?

Are there any areas of your life that you think God cannot restore?

Find Scriptures that build your faith over fear in each area.

Read **Week 12 – Your Battle Cry**
if fear is trying to enter into your heart.

The LORD is my light and my salvation; whom shall I fear?
the LORD is the strength of my life; of whom shall I be afraid?
– Psalms 27:1

Week 11: *Your Army*

๛

Joshua 23:10
One man of you shall chase a thousand:
for the Lord your God, he it is that fighteth for you,
as he hath promised you.

๛

The issues in the world we live in can sometimes be overwhelming. At times, you may feel outnumbered, outsmarted or depressed by the circumstances surrounding you. It is in these times of weakness that God fights for you. He is your army, your military force and your secret weapon. He fights for you in the spiritual realm which manifests in the natural realm. He can easily conquer wickedness, sickness and even generational curses. He fights hidden enemies that you cannot yet see. No matter what you come up against or how great the opposition may seem, God is already there. He is all you need.

This week's Scripture is Joshua giving a warning to love God and stay close to Him because He fights for you.

Joshua explains that with God, one man can defeat a thousand men on earth. Those are some good odds. Do you feel as though you have the natural strength to take on one thousand opponents all at once? When you are with God, you are actually that powerful. You may feel that the enemy has surrounded you in great numbers or, that the enemy is greater in power, expertise, backing or influence. However, the enemy's opposition is no match for your power with God. He promises to take care of anything or anyone that opposes His own children. His power becomes your strength and force. God will combat any adversary, of any magnitude, on your behalf.

So how do you access God's army and connect with His power?

Stay close to God. Sometimes, you cannot immediately see or feel God's presence in difficult situations or while under extreme pressure. Meditating Scriptures on this topic will assure you of His promise to be your army and fight for you. It requires faith and your absolute trust in His ability.

My trust in God increased when I found myself in a horrific battle against darkness. I was entangled with wickedness that tried to destroy everything I had and steal my joy. It wanted to scar me with betrayal. At first, the lies and deceptions appeared mightier than the truth and I was very confused. I did not know how or where to begin to fight. There was nothing I could take, drink, smoke or do to get relief from this painful situation – I was numb. I soon realized, there was absolutely nothing in this world, or anyone on the planet who could help me, heal me or restore me. I felt alone and defenseless - or at least I thought. Once I finally came to the end of myself, I surrendered the situation over to God.

I went into the Bible and sought out Scriptures dealing with fighting an enemy. I meditated on them until they stayed inside my heart. I repeated them out loud until I had eliminated any doubt of loneliness. Finally, I had arrived at the place where I truly believed God would fight this battle for me. He told me to focus on Him and walk in faith.

Before the situation got better, it went from bad to worse. The enemy seemed to be getting more vicious with my demise. All that I had in life, or thought I had, was completely destroyed in a matter of days. I was destitute, but I never stopped meditating on the Word and staying focused on God. His promises were the only things still intact in my life. I was determined to continue my good fight of faith.

*Trust in the LORD with all thine heart;
and lean not unto thine own understanding.* **- Proverbs 3:5**

My natural eyes could not see God's army fighting on my behalf, but my faith knew His army was active behind the scenes. His army was able to go into places where I had no access - right into the enemy's camp. He knew their evil schemes and could see through their dark secrets. There was no way I could have fought on so many fronts all at the same time. Besides, I was emotionally and financially depleted. God turned everything that was used against me into something that was used for my good. It was like I had an army of skilled warriors, angels, and comrades on the front line assaulting my enemies while protecting me at the same time. Letting God handle my situation transformed a ridiculous mess into a perfect testimony of His power.

And the Lord shall utter his voice before his army:
for his camp is very great: for he is strong that executeth his word:
for the day of the Lord is great and very terrible;
*and who can abide it? – **Joel 2:11***

Reflecting back, I wish I sought out God sooner. No one but God can take the credit for my deliverance out of a deep pit of despair. I greatly appreciate how He revealed another dimension of His love and power to me that I never knew before. I connected to His power when I put my complete trust in Him and relinquished my own efforts. What a relief! No more anxiety. No more fear. Imagine the joy and amazement I felt. In the end, I came out of a horrible situation better than I was before.

God promises to fight for you. Whether it is finances, health, relationships or anything you face, put His army to work for you. There are principalities that you may not be aware of initiating an attack against you. There may be people you consider friends who are not for you. God knows all and can see everything. He can give you the power of a thousand men at one time. He equips you for every confrontation you will ever face. Trust and believe that God's power will fight for you!

> Remain close to God and trust Him to provide the power of an army!

Journal Reflections

Read Joshua Chapter 23 in its entirety.
Describe a time in your life where you felt outnumbered, outsmarted or overwhelmed in a situation.
How did you handle these types of situations in the past?
Explain how you will prepare for these types of situations in the future.
Why is it important to allow God to fight for you?
Do you believe and trust that He will?
How can you grow closer and remain close to God?

Week 12: *Your Battle Cry*

Psalm 27:6
And now shall mine head be lifted up
above mine enemies round about me:
therefore will I offer in his tabernacle sacrifices of joy;
I will sing, yea, I will sing praises unto the Lord

Praise is very necessary. It precedes victory and stirs up faith. There are so many statistics about the influence of music. You probably have experienced how a certain song affects your mood and gets you going. You may have witnessed how songs can set the tone in certain environments. A simple song can create energy and evoke emotions.

Remember how some secular music made you feel? Listening to "hype" songs before an intense workout or competition produced an adrenelin rush throughout your body. Certain lyrics actually evoked emotions such as passion, sadness, contentment, joy, anger and even lust. Have you ever caught yourself singing a song that you had not heard in years? It is amazing how your subconsious can recall words that have been set to music. Words are very powerful and music provides a melodic entry into your spirit. Unfortunately, mainstream music does not give many examples or selections of good praise.

This week's Scripture shares words of wisdom from David. He tells of guaranteed triumph over your enemies when you offer joy unto the Lord through songs of praise.

***Praise** (verb): to extol in words or song; to magnify;*
to glorify on account of perfections or excellent works;
to do honor to; to display the excellence of

When should you praise?

You should praise in the midst of a battle...when you get a bad doctor's report, an excessive bill, or unfavorable news about a family member. You should praise when you have conflict in your personal relationships, professional connections, business affairs or community relations. You should praise when people have hurt you and turned their back on you. You should also praise when you are recovering from surgery, from loss, from rejection or from daily stress. You should especially praise when you find yourself in a dark pit of discouragement, grief, depression or despair. You praise anytime you feel like you are under attack. It is during these difficult times of painful emotions when you must open your mouth and *sing* praise. You cannot think praise in your mind. It requires your vocal cords to release praise into the atmosphere. Not only do you praise when you are low, you also praise in joyful times. You are extremely powerful when you choose to praise during any situation.

Singing praises is another method of building your faith. It calms your spirit and eliminates fear. In addition, by praising God, you also build your spiritual strength. There are many genres of praise music that can complement your personal style. I urge you to invest in your favorite type of praise music this week to help guide and encourage you in your time of worship. Take time to find praise music that you enjoy. You can even make up a simple praise song to sing at any given occasion. Your own personal praise selections are useful when you are in a place where the only music available is the music coming out of your heart. You can even sing Scriptures aloud as praise. Here are examples of simple praise words you can sing to your own melody...

God, I thank you for the victory! Hal-le-lu-jah!
I thank you for the victory! Hal-le-lu-jah!

Greater is He – That's in Me – Than he that's in the world.

Jesus loves me. God is love.
Jesus loves me. God is love.

It is good to sing praises every day for any reason you can find. Praise is a celebration that will open your heart to God.

Praise is something Christians are purposed to do. It is an act of love, respect, honor and admiration to the Most Worthy, God Almighty. Praise creates an atmosphere for His presence to enter in. It is a form of thanksgiving and exalts your trust in Him. Praise also brings terror to the enemy and puts him on notice of his defeat. It motivates your angels to work on your behalf. God loves to hear your songs of praise. Praise is powerful - it is a battle cry of triumph! Let praises continually come out of your mouth.

Welcome God's power in your life through songs of praise!

Therefore will I give thanks unto thee, O LORD, among the heathen, and sing praises unto thy name. **- Psalm 18:49**

Journal Reflections

Read Psalm Chapter 27 in its entirety.

What secular songs bring you joy, inspiration or motivation?

What have you been praising in place of God?

What are the Gospel stations in your area?

What words in Scripture encourage you?

If you had to make up your own praise song, what would the lyrics be?

Search for a Gospel song/artist that has similar lyrics.

Week 13: *Encouragement*

ಐಖ

1 John 4:4
*Ye are of God, little children, and have overcome them:
because greater is he that is in you,
than he that is in the world.*

ಐಖ

Encouragement inspires and motivates. It causes hope to expand and increases confidence. Encouragement always helps you to take action, move forward and reach higher. It contributes to the progress of growth in your life. There is a positive force within encouragement that your spirit acknowledges.

Having an arsenal of encouragement readily available will prove to be beneficial during spiritual warfare. In your darkest hour, others may be at a loss for words or in need of encouragement themselves. You do not have to depend on others for comfort or inspiration. Along with praise, you can find Scriptures that provide encouragement to you during a season of trials and tribulations. These Scriptures can become your "power" Scriptures because they come straight from the Word of God. They consistently provide encouragement, love and strength when you speak them out of your own mouth.

Overcome (verb): to conquer; to vanquish; to subdue; to win a victory over

Greater (adjective): denoting more magnitude or extension than something else, or beyond what is usual; vast; extensive; magnanimous; superior

This week's Scripture is a simple reminder that you are a beloved child of God and have overcome the world.

It can be a great power scripture for you to meditate on when you need to be uplifted or re-energized. It expresses the following:

1. You are of God
2. God is in you
3. You (and God in you) have victory over all the evil in this world
4. God is far superior to anything you will encounter in this world

The Word of God says you *have* overcome the world. It is already done. Wow! There is no force of nature, wickedness, witchcraft, curses, strongholds, diseases, or depression - past, present or future - that is too great for God who dwells within you. You do not have to be afraid or worried anymore. Nothing and no one in this world can come against you and win! Unless you surrender to an evil adversary, your outcome will always be victorious. There can be no doubt that God is in you and He is for you.

> *What shall we then say to these things? If God be for us, who can be against us?* – **Romans 8:31**

Life sometimes brings daggers that pierce you all at once. Hardships may become unbearable and take you to a point where you have no energy to fight. You can become so depleted that you forget the greatness that dwells inside of your spirit. Meditating on this Scripture, and others like it, can bring you out of depression or a defeated attitude. It will remind you of the abundant source of power that you are associated with and will encourage you. The vision of your future success is once again re-ignited. The more you meditate, the more reassured you are. In just a few days, you can be at peace with all anxiety eliminated - all of this from just one Scripture!

You have probably heard accounts of modern day miracles; stories of people overcoming life-threatening diseases, those who have endured horrific personal experiences or who have survived natural disasters. Their testimonies are amazing! They explain how God saved, delivered and restored them. Despite a mighty opposition, they ended up in a better place than anyone could have ever imagined. They connected with the greater power of God. No matter what their circumstances, they were able to remain encouraged and overcome it. God wants to encourage you and remind you that He is with you, especially when you feel weak or overwhelmed. He wants you to know that you can overcome anything. He is the greater power within you.

Encourage yourself with the Word of God!

Journal Reflections

Read 1 John Chapter 4 in its entirety.
What or who gives you the most encouragement?
How do you encourage others?
Describe an experience where you overcame something with God.
Is there anything in the world that you feel is greater than you? Explain.
How can the Word of God encourage you to victory?
What Scriptures would you consider to be your power Scriptures?

Week 14: *Power of the Tongue*

ಸಿಂಡ

Proverbs 18:21
Death and life are in the power of the tongue:
and they that love it shall eat the fruit thereof.

ಸಿಂಡ

Many doctrines and teachings agree on the extraordinary power words have in this world. Regardless of the spiritual belief, words are considered to have an enormous ability to control the atmosphere in which one lives. Words seem to have an universal effect on people regardless of race, status, gender or age. Words inspire and motivate, and they can also hurt and degrade. Words have the power to release a blessing or unleash a curse.

This week's Scripture explains the two opposing forces - death and life - which come from the words of your tongue.

Death *(noun): the permanent end of all life functions in an organism; destruction; extinction*

Death is more than just the demise of a human being. It is an elimination of dreams, love, confidence, happiness and all positive experiences. Words that are associated with death are toxic - they boost fear and hopelessness.

Here are a few examples of words filled with death:

"You're killing me"   "F--- you" "F--- me"

"I will never forgive them"   "I'm sick and tired of…"

"I can't do anything…"   "I don't need you"

"Nothing good ever happens to me"   "That won't work"

"Who cares"   "You are worthless and nothing to me"

"Whatever"   "If it ain't one thing, it's another"

"You're never going to amount to anything"

"I'm not good enough"   "Take it and shut up"

"You are a *%#!"   "You're not that special"

"That disease runs in my family"   "No one loves you"

"Life's a @!&#, then you die"   "Just give up"

"You get on my last nerve"   "I hate you"

Life (noun): animation and energy in action or expression; nourishment; supreme felicity; the condition of living or the state of being alive

Life creates and brings forth positive energy into the atmosphere. When life is activated, it expands, motivates and multiplies. Words that bring life possess faith.

Here are a few examples of words filled with life:

"You're the best" "Dream big"

"You can do it" "Great job" "This is our time"

"Anything is possible" "I appreciate you"

"I am healed and healthy beyond measure"

"Prosperity and good success is ours"

"I trust you" "I am proud of you"

"You're a great… (friend, dad, mom, spouse)"

"No matter what, I am with you" "Great idea"

"Life is good" "We will get through this"

"Thank you very much" "All is well"

"I hope the best for you" "You are beautiful"

"Keep up the good work" "I love you"

If you like to talk, (...*they that love it*) you have to be especially careful to choose the correct words with the right intentions. It takes temperance not to use words sarcastically, say words under your breath or unleash words in reaction to heightened emotional states. Words arranged for comic relief and idle words are especially dangerous since they appear to be insignificant or "just silly talk." Even if you justify your words based on circumstances, it does not change their impact.

The power of words is often forgotten and most always underestimated. Whatever is spoken, death or life, you *will* reap the result (...*shall eat the fruit thereof*). No matter how your words are used or what they are used for, they will manifest what is spoken. If you want to change your situation, speak words of newness and transformation. Do not continue to speak the current state of affairs in your life. Stop bringing up past pain, hurt and regret. They will only continue to manifest in your life. Instead, fill your mouth with words of restoration, love, healing and life. It is a difficult process in the beginning. If you do not know what to say, just repeat the promises of God, "I'm healed...I'm blessed...I'm more than a conqueror...I'm filled with joy." Soon, you will be more specific with your words of life.

I heard one pastor say - we should all be thankful that God has not yet turned up the power gauge over the words we speak. He said most of us have to operate at setting one, instead of at the highest setting of ten. He further explained that if the gauge was set at ten and every word spoken out of our mouths instantly occurred, we would have already killed ourselves and everyone around us. Cuss words, exaggerations, words of wrath or bitterness, lies and words spoken in fear would all manifest in our lives. As a result of our recklessness with words, we live at a lower setting. Our tongue does not function with the power it was created to have. God has to protect us from ourselves until we learn to speak words of life in every situation.

> *Let no corrupt communication proceed out of your mouth,*
> *but that which is good to the use of edifying,*
> *that it may minister grace unto the hearers*
> *– **Ephesians 4:29***

Once you master speaking life, inspired from the Word of God, your power gauge can be turned up. You will experience a positive transformation from within. True power is the ability to bring life to everything around you.

Use your tongue to speak powerful words of life!

Journal Reflections

Read Proverbs Chapter 18 in its entirety.

What is your tongue producing – life or death? Explain.

What words do you say to yourself?

What words do you speak to describe the person(s) closest to you?

How can you add new words of life to your vocabulary?

What Scripture(s) can you begin speaking over your life?

Week 15: *Good Ground*

☙❧

Matthew 13:23
But he that received seed into the good ground is he that heareth the Word, and understandeth it; which also beareth fruit, and bringeth forth, some an hundredfold, some sixty, some thirty.

☙❧

Farming cultivates plants and other life forms. It is necessary to generate food for the purpose of sustaining life. The condition of the soil is very important to yield the best crops. Different types of soil and climates, specific to each crop, determine how much harvest will be produced. Just planting a seed is not enough. Experienced farmers take care to cultivate the soil prior to planting seeds. They take care to prepare good ground - ground which is suitable, healthy and ready to receive.

This week's Scripture is Jesus speaking about the sower of the seed (the Word of God). He describes good ground as a sower (a person) who hears the Word and understands it.

Good ground brings forth a plentiful harvest. For one seed, thirty, sixty or a hundred "fruits" are produced. Ask any farmer - that is a great harvest. As Believers, there is one fundamental aspect to being *the good ground*...understanding. You prepare the ground of your heart to reap a supernatural harvest by truly understanding the seed, which is the Word of God.

Do you understand the Word of God?

> ***Understanding*** *(noun): apprehending the ideas or sense of another; knowledge; exact comprehension; discernment*

Take care to read God's Word and meditate on it until it speaks to your spirit. Revelation on what He is specifically saying to you will be received. You will produce "fruit" or actual results that correspond to the Word of God you hear, believe, obey and understand.

For comparison, let's take a look at preceding Scriptures that describe three types of ground that do not produce fruit at all.

The Way Side (no ground at all)

> *When any one heareth the word of the kingdom,*
> *and understandeth it not, then cometh the wicked one,*
> *and catcheth away that which was sown in his heart.*
> *This is he which received seed by the way side.*
> *– Matthew 13:19*

This describes a person who has no comprehension of the Scriptures or how to apply it in their life. When they hear the Word of God, they do not understand it. This disconnect is usually caused by not seeking Him for themselves and not having a personal relationship with their Heavenly Father. Consequently, there is no available ground in his or her heart that is prepared to receive. Any seeds of the Word are scattered about for Satan to steal. Along the way side, there is no ground or soil for the seed to begin to grow.

Stony Places (ground of stones and gravel)

> *But he that received the seed into stony places, the same is he that*
> *heareth the word, and anon with joy receiveth it;*
> *Yet hath he not root in himself, but dureth for a while:*
> *for when tribulation or persecution ariseth because of the word,*
> *by and by he is offended. – Matthew 13:20-21*

This describes a person who is excited when they first hear the Word of God. They may partially understand it and can apply it in their lives during good times. But, as soon as times of adversity and tribulation come, they become angry with God and disconnect with the Kingdom. They have available ground, but their seeds do not grow deep roots. Roots are needed to stay connected with His promises when circumstances are not favorable. Without deep roots, doubt and fear smother the seed. Offense or frustration hardens their hearts to stone where seeds need to grow. This condition is usually caused by little faith and can be overcome with consistent fellowship with God. However, in stony places, the ground is too hard for roots to establish and produce fruit.

Among the Thorns (ground full of weeds and thorny plants)

He also that received seed among the thorns is he that heareth the word; and the care of this world, and the deceitfulness of riches, choke the word, and he becometh unfruitful.
– Matthew 13:22

This describes a person who hears the Word of God and receives it, but allows worry and fear to consume them. Their ground is available and suitable for seeds to produce roots, but soon becomes infested with weeds of worry. Their fear causes anxiety which can compel them to entertain get-rich-quick schemes the world offers. Weeds strangle any Word of God from abounding in their heart. Weeds block truth, love and light and quickly become oppressive. As a result, the seeds suffocate because they are not receiving continuous nourishment and light from unyielding faith. Ground full of thorny plants or weeds, suffocate seeds and cause them to become unfruitful.

So how can you have good ground?

Here are some ways to help prepare the soil of your heart:

1. **Survey the ground of your heart.** Are you saved and ready to receive the Word of God?

2. **Pull up all weeds and clear away all stones.** Pray for assistance from the Holy Spirit to help excavate your heart so that fresh, new soil can fill it.

3. **Begin seeking and studying the Word of God in different versions.** Use a Bible concordance to assist you in your understanding of the Word of God and His Kingdom principles.

4. **Meditate the Word of God to cultivate the Word within you.** Confess you are good ground.

   *Make me to understand the way of thy precepts:
   so shall I talk of thy wondrous works.* – **Psalm 119:27**

5. **Pray and fellowship with God daily.** This will deepen your relationship with Him and build your faith to do all things.

Hearing the Word alone is not enough. The Word of God, without understanding, cannot produce results. It is like hearing directions, but in a language foreign to you. The directions are accurate and will get you to your destination, but until you actually understand the language, you won't be able to follow them. You must seek to understand the Word of God. When you gain understanding, you receive seed into good ground. You are ready to reap a harvest of thirty, sixty and hundredfold. A harvest of a hundredfold is far more than 100%, it is a 1 to 100 ratio. In other words, for every one seed you plant, you will reap a harvest of 100 fruit. With good ground, you will bear fruit of supernatural results. Your harvest will be greater than you ever imagined!

Understand the Word of God and the more fruitful, the more faithful, and the more powerful you become!

Journal Reflections

Read Matthew Chapter 13 in its entirety.
How would you describe the "ground" in your heart?
What steals or smothers your seed when you hear the Word of God?
How can you increase the quality of your soil?
What do you understand about God and His Son, Jesus?
Research specific Scriptures or topics you would like to gain a better understanding of. Pray for wisdom and revelation while you seek the Word of God.

Week 16: *Forgiveness*

ॐ

Ephesians 4:32
*And be ye kind one to another,
tenderhearted, forgiving one another,
even as God for Christ's sake
hath forgiven you.*

ॐ

Forgiveness is a transforming and liberating choice. Yet, forgiveness is one decision many people have difficulty making. When people hurt you, it can pierce the heart permanently if you do not let go of the anger. Pain from an unjust wrong can be so traumatic that you hold lasting grudges or plot revenge against those who have hurt you. You may have convinced yourself that certain negative situations, events or words spoken against you are unforgivable.

Examples of experiences that people struggle with forgiveness are:

- Cheating
- Molestation or Rape
- Betrayal
- Stealing
- Murder
- Divorce
- Lying
- Rejection, Abandonment or Neglect
- Abuse – Physical or Mental

These negative experiences and those not mentioned, can grip your emotions and take power away from you. If you do not forgive, the pain will take you down a dark path of bitterness, vengeance, resentment and even depression.

This week's Scripture is Paul advising you to forgive others as God forgave you through Jesus Christ.

In addition to forgiveness, you should be kind and tenderhearted to one another. To be all three, at the same time, is definitely a walk in faith.

Kind (adjective): having tenderness or goodness of nature; benevolent; having or showing a considerate and helpful nature; generously responsive

Tenderhearted (adjective): easily moved to love

Forgiving (adjective): inclined to overlook offenses; merciful; compassionate; pardoning; remitting

You may be asking yourself how you can be considerate and sympathetic to undeserving, cruel people. How can you forgive those who are evil and mean without a cause? Well, forgiveness is for you – not for them. People who hurt you have had an evil spirit operating through them. Evil does not care who it hurts and does not care if you forgive it or not. Forgiveness *releases you* from the bondage of hurt and pain. Forgiveness ceases any torment evil has over you and empowers you to overcome negative emotions. There are many statistics showing the health benefits of forgiveness, but above all else, God commands you to forgive.

After hearing a sermon about forgiveness one day, I decided to write down all the people who had hurt me and all who I had not yet forgiven. I shared each name and incidence with God. I re-lived and re-capped every offense to justify why I never forgave them. God held me in His arms as I poured out my deepest heartaches. The more I let out, the more people came to my remembrance that I needed to forgive. This process uncovered that I had never truly forgiven my parents for their divorce. Although they have always been supportive and loving, I was disappointed by them for quitting on each other. Even into adulthood, I resented splitting holidays, family and special events between the two people I cherished most. I realized that this tiny chip of bitterness on my shoulder needed to be removed with forgiveness so I could move on with my life.

This time alone with Him revealed I had also been holding on to other people's unforgiveness. I should not have been carrying their afflictions at all. I still felt anger towards people who hurt my close friends, family members and even my friends' family members. How did I have room enough in my heart to harbor the extra pain of others? Tears flowed uncontrollably when I told God I was giving up all the grudges and my hardness of heart that day. I decided to forgive everyone – including those who never apologized - that was probably the hardest.

The closest physical comparison I can think of is the time I got the wind knocked out of me while playing soccer. Somehow, the ball was kicked directly into my stomach at close range. I could see and hear everything around me, but I could not breathe. My entire body felt weak as I collapsed to the ground waiting for the pain to pass so I could breathe again. That is sort of what it felt like to forgive everyone in one huge batch.

However, once I forgave everyone, I felt a freedom and healing inside my spirit. I realized it was not the people who upset me, but dark principalities that used them to keep me under the control and burden of emotional baggage. It was a ploy to keep my heart cluttered and disconnected from God. I was grateful to finally be free!

You can be free and healed of affliction, too. Pain and sorrow is not the life God intended for you. Forgiving others is important for your spiritual growth. It opens your heart and gives you the ability to be kind and tenderhearted. Without forgiveness, it is impossible to treat others with compassion. After you forgive others, you must also forgive yourself. This forgiveness is imperative for moving forward with God. You must see yourself how He sees you...spotless, pure, full of love and forgiven. Forgiving yourself causes regrets to dissolve away. It eliminates any bondage to guilt and shame, anger and bitterness that want to steal your joy.

Do not focus on what will happen to those who have hurt you. Once you forgive and release the anger, God can come in with vengeance and recompense as He said in His Word.

Vengeance (noun): infliction of pain on another, in return for an injury or offense; retribution; revenge

Recompense (verb): to compensate; to make return of an equivalent for anything given, done or suffered; to return an equivalent; to repay

ುಲ ಓ

*Dearly beloved, avenge not yourselves, but rather give place unto (God's) wrath: for it is written, Vengeance is mine; I will repay, saith the Lord. – **Romans 12:19***

*Seeing it is a righteous thing with God to recompense tribulation to them that trouble you; - **2 Thessalonians 1:6***

You should never take vengeance into your own hands. It will harden your heart and entice you into darkness. You are not the almighty judge. Even more so, you are not equipped to administer a proper sentence. Only God knows the heart of mankind and the spirits working through them. He can turn any bad situation into something that works for your good. He knows how to deal with all things that hurt you, but only when you forgive and allow Him to take over.

Being kind, tenderhearted and forgiving builds your confidence in God's love. You do not have to worry about getting hurt and living in bondage ever again. You know the power of forgiveness and can move forward in life. You understand that your feelings will sometimes get bruised temporarily, but you believe God to administer His justice to your adversaries. Your relationship with Him grows to another level of trust and intimacy. You may have to battle with your emotions to forgive, but it is worth your freedom. Forgiving others is your victory over darkness.

No forgiveness, no power!

Journal Reflections
Read Ephesians Chapter 4 in its entirety.
Who are the people in your life that you need to forgive?
How will your life change if you do forgive?
What will happen if you do not forgive?
Do you need to forgive yourself?
How can you increase in kindness and tenderheartedness?
Who or what do you think can hurt you now?
Why do you think God always forgives you?

Week 17: *Healing*

※

Acts 10:38
*How God anointed Jesus of Nazareth
with the Holy Ghost and with power:
who went about doing good,
and healing all that were oppressed of the devil;
for God was with him.*

※

In these times, it appears the whole world needs healing. Countries are at war among its citizens and government. Leaders are succumbing to the pressures of corruption. Families are becoming dysfunctional and disconnected from God. Our young people are becoming desensitized to ungodliness and violence. The pestilence, sin and suffering found in the far corners of the earth are now close to home. It is evident that Satan is trying to infiltrate our lives with heartache and agony. He wants to convince us we live in a fallen world where there is no hope. Thankfully, there is healing available to all and for all situations. Healing cleanses and frees us from evil. It comes with the power to restore a person, a family, a community – even the entire world.

This week's Scripture is a reminder of the anointing and power God gave to Jesus to heal others, just as He has given you as a Believer.

While Jesus walked the earth, He did not hesitate to heal everyone. Whether it was physical, mental or spiritual infirmities, Jesus healed them all. When Jesus was crucified for your sins, His shed blood also healed you of all your infirmities, now and forever. There will never be anything that cannot be healed through God and the blood of Jesus.

Heal (verb): to cure of a disease or wound and restore to soundness; to purify from corruptions, redress grievances and restore to prosperity; make healthy again

Who his own self bare our sins in his own body on the tree, that we, being dead to sins, should live unto righteousness: by whose stripes ye were healed. **– 1 Peter 2:24**

Healing is important.

Think about how the world would be if it was void of healing. What a miserable place it would be. Past hurts, diseases, pain and present circumstances would never go away. You would have to carry the weight of suffering all by yourself. Not a day would go by without a negative comment or reaction to wounds that never healed. You would need healing in your physical body, as well as, healing for the afflictions of the heart and mind. Thank God for His healing power and for sending Jesus to heal you from all attacks of the devil. Healing is important so that you can move on to the future God has for you. He does not want you to dwell in the past or remain stuck in present circumstances. Healing increases self-esteem, physical and mental health which improves how you interact with others. It makes you whole and sets you free from oppression. Healing brings inner joy and a peace that only comes from Jesus.

Healing covers all.

Jesus not only died for your sins, but he bore all of your infirmities and any oppression unleashed from the devil. His healing covers all things, in any area of life.

Healing covers these areas below, but not limited to:

- a broken heart
- demonic possession
- lust and addictions
- mental disorders or emotional distress
- any type of disease or physical condition
- generational curses
- loss of any kind – person, job, home, limb, etc.
- betrayal and deception
- shame from personal actions or the actions of others against you

Healing is for all who believe.

God wants to heal everyone, but only few will believe in Him and His son, Jesus. He hears His children and responds.

> *O Lord my God, I cried unto thee,*
> *and thou hast healed me. - **Psalm 30:2***

When you accept the truth of His Word, healing can manifest. God has already provided healing and wants you to receive it for yourself. You must cultivate His healing power within your spirit and maintain patience. As you mature in your healing power and grow in confidence, you will want to help others. God gives you this anointing to heal others if you believe.

> *And these signs shall follow them that believe; In my name shall they cast out devils; they shall speak with new tongues; They shall take up serpents; and if they drink any deadly thing, it shall not hurt them; they shall lay hands on the sick, and they shall recover.*
> *– Mark 16:17-18*

You do not use the power of healing to test God. Some people have purposely drank poison, denied themselves or others medicine, or put themselves in harm's way as a test of His healing power. These acts are not what He intended for healing. Healing is for those who have been attacked by demons inflicting sickness, pain and torment over them. Prayer and close fellowship with God will give you the wisdom needed to properly administer healing.

Healing comes from God through Jesus.

Some think healing comes through modern medicine, sorcery, psychiatry or even their own personal efforts. They do not believe that Jesus already paid the price for their healing. They have not received their healing because they think it must be paid for again. Any source of healing outside of God is a counterfeit and will not last. It may look like a form of healing in the beginning, but it does not have the irreversible, everlasting and restorative power that only comes from God through Jesus. His son, Jesus, was crucified for your sins and the blood He shed paid the price for your healing.

You may ask, if healing comes from God, should I go to the doctor or take medicine? *Yes*. Doctors are specifically trained to detect diseases, intrusions, dysfunctions and misalignments in your body. Many doctors are anointed with a natural gift to aid the sick and restore health to their patients. They help you to understand unfamiliar territories of the body that are in need of healing. Doctors prescribe medicine or therapy to ease the pain and support you while you manifest your healing. Doctors are necessary, but God is the cure. He is the One who already healed you and made you whole.

>Receive your complete healing that Jesus
>already paid the price for!

Journal Reflections

Read Acts Chapter 10 in its entirety.

This week, also read Matthew Chapters 8 and 9.

What areas of your life are you in need of healing?

Describe how your life will change once you are healed in those areas.

Find Scriptures that address healing in your areas of need.

How can you increase your faith for healing from God?

Week 18: *Grace and Glory*

ℬℭ

Psalm 84:11
For the Lord God is a sun and shield:
the Lord will give grace and glory:
no good thing will he withhold
from them that walk uprightly.

ℬℭ

All undeserved privileges and divine favor can be considered as grace. Good things that are extended to us without any effort on our part are examples of how grace impacts our lives. Grace is not just a covering over our sins; it is also a source of power.

Grace *(noun): the free and unmerited favor and love of God; good will; kindness; favorable influence of God; privilege; excellence*

Glory *(noun): brightness; luster; splendor; magnificence; praise; high honor; honorable representation of God*

This week's Scripture is part of a sacred song in the book of Psalms. It is gives praise to God and expresses the joy that comes with living for Him

It says that the Lord will protect you and give you light. You will receive free and unmerited favor along with His honor. As you live in the integrity and excellence of Him, no good thing will be withheld from you.

The result of grace means you always have what you need in all circumstances. You are well supplied to do any and every thing to accomplish a multitude of good works. Some define grace as the blessing of God. The Amplified Bible defines grace as God supplying you always with all sufficiency to require no aid or support from the outside world. Grace covers everything you need to be successful. So grace is more than forgiveness and mercy. It is the "all-inclusive" power to get positive results in your life.

Positive results are the good things in life that produce righteous success to take care of all your needs. Positive results, through the power of God, are in such abundance that you will have more than enough to help others. You have no worries or cares. He is always ready to protect and guide you through any circumstance. The Lord is your light in the darkness. He is your splendor when you feel down or unworthy.

You may understand what it is like to fight the fear of running out or being overwhelmed by thoughts of financial loss and economic uncertainties. During difficult times, it is hard not to look around and begin to take notice of the things you do not have. It seems as if you cannot keep up with life's demands. On top of that, Satan tries to make you feel unqualified, unworthy, and incapable of doing anything of significance. He wants to keep you focused on present conditions and past mistakes to deter you from your successful future. You may feel you have done all you know how to do, but nothing seems to work. It is times like these that you can appreciate the grace and glory of God.

> *But thou, O LORD, art a shield for me; my glory, and the lifter up of mine head.* **– Psalm 3:3**

God wants to take care of all your needs, responsibilities and dreams. The more you spend time with Him, the more your mind renews to Kingdom principles. Your desires become aligned with the desires He has for you. While you grow in His Word, grace covers any mistakes or shortcomings. He knows you are not perfect, but you are still His precious child. He extends grace so you can receive favor and undeserved privileges on your journey. He extends glory so that you can shine brightly in the midst of tribulation and darkness. Others will see the good results in your life and want to know more about the loving God you serve.

How can you experience God's grace and glory?

Live righteously and live by faith. Trust God, believe and obey His Word. Cultivate a personal relationship with your Heavenly Father. Live like you are an heir to the most powerful and most gracious royal family. No matter what has happened in the past, you are regarded as honorable, strong, prosperous and kind. Grace empowers you with confidence to move forward. Glory strengthens you to live boldly for Him. Both are for the new challenges, the new beginnings and your new life in Christ. God wants you to live a life full of abundance, goodness and positive results!

Therefore, as ye abound in every thing, in faith, and utterance, and knowledge, and in all diligence, and in your love to us, see that ye abound in this grace also.– **2 Corinthians 8:7**

Walk with integrity and experience the power
of grace and glory!

Journal Reflections
Read Psalm Chapter 84 in its entirety.
Why is it important for the Lord God to give you grace and glory?
Who do you extend grace and glory to? Why?
What areas of your life would you like more grace?
How can you increase in your trust and obedience to God?
What does it mean to you to live a life of faith, integrity and righteousness?

Week 19: *Sow*

Galatians 6:7-8
*Be not deceived; God is not mocked:
for whatsoever a man soweth, that shall he also reap.
For he that soweth to his flesh
shall of the flesh reap corruption;
but he that soweth to the Spirit
shall of the Spirit reap life everlasting.*

What goes around comes around, right? Receiving what you have given out is a common principle in many cultures and religions. On the contrary, evil does not take heed to this principle at all. It wreaks havoc in the lives of others without regard to consequence or retribution. Throughout the Bible and in world history, wickedness strives to utterly destroy any and all who stand up against it. Although it has terrorized many, evil seems to overlook those with a divine destiny. There is always one, who against all odds, defeats wickedness and comes out as the victor. In the very end, evil reaps what it has sown.

This week's Scripture speaks as a friendly reminder and simple warning: God is real and every action has a consequence.

God is not to be mocked. What you sow, you will reap. It is interesting that this Scripture begins by stating *"be not deceived."* Do not be misled. It wants you to be aware of the deception that tries to conceal the truth about God, His power and reaping what you sow. God and His principles are not to be mimicked, defied or treated with contempt.

***Deceive** (verb): to ensnare; be false to; be dishonest with; cause someone to believe an untruth or disbelieve what is true*

***Mock** (verb): to imitate or mimic in contempt or derision; to ridicule; to treat with scorn; to disappoint*

Who would mock God?

Those who mock Him worship wickedness, challenge or defy His power and disgrace the Word of God through blasphemy. Too often, some baby Christians treat God with disrespect when they act and speak in willful disobedience to His Word. Unfortunately, there are those who try to imitate Him by ruling over others – abusers, tyrants, false prophets, cult leaders, etc.

The Scripture goes on to explain a very important spiritual principle: whatever you sow, you will reap.

Simply put, the words and deeds you do today will produce an associated result in the future. This concept is not complicated, yet it is often disregarded. You may have spoken words and done things that you inwardly know you do not want to reap the associated harvest in return. In these cases, you have to repent and ask God to allow you to uproot some of your seeds. Your repentance and obedience to Him grants you grace to change your harvest.

Sow (verb): plant seeds in or on the ground for future growth; introduce into an environment

Reap (verb): to gather; to obtain; to receive as a reward, or as the fruit of labor or of works; in a good or bad sense; to get or derive

Mean and evil people do not regard the principle of sowing and reaping. They assume that what they are doing to others cannot possibly be done back to them. For example, an adult may feel that if they molest a child, they cannot be molested because they are too old. Or a corporate boss who abuses their staff and degrades them may feel that they, themselves, will never be in a position to reap that particular harvest. What they do not realize is that the harvest reaped, is not always the exact measure or way in which it was sown. They are deceived and underestimate the everlasting power of God's principle. One sinful seed can reap a variety of harvests including: guilt, incarceration, financial ruin, torment, death, disease, etc.

Sowing and reaping is an established principle similar to the law of gravity. It cares nothing of the type of person who jumps off a cliff. Whether you are nice, mean, smart, ignorant, Christian or heathen; the law still applies. Gravity will always cause you to fall down to the earth. Likewise, you will always reap what you sow, regardless of who you are or what you believe.

The world has no regard for Godly standards. It glorifies eating what you want, saying what you think and acting in accordance to how your flesh feels right now. The world encourages living for self, instead of living for God. It persuades you to live in the moment and take no thought about the consequences you must face in the future. It does not care if you go to hell tomorrow - at least you had fun today. You have to be mindful of the timeless principle of sowing and reaping regardless of what is going on around you. The world does not want you to believe that you will ever reap a harvest - good or bad. If it appears that evil is not reaping, have patience, harvest time will come. You must always remember that whatever you do or *sow*, even in the privacy of your own home or secret assembly, you will still reap a harvest.

*Even as I have seen, they that plow iniquity,
and sow wickedness, reap the same. – **Job 4:8***

Sowing is a very important principle in the Kingdom of God. It is mentioned several times throughout the Bible in both the Old and New Testament - there are no contradictions. When you understand this principle, live righteously, and sow bountifully in the things of God, your harvest will be plentiful. You become confident about your future and can expect an abundant return with every seed.

> Sow bountifully in the things of God
> and reap its power!

Journal Reflections

*Read Galatians Chapter 6 in its entirety.
What type of seeds do you sow into your family?
Your peers? Your job?
Are there any seeds that you should repent for?
Explain and repent.
What type of harvest would you like to see in your life?
How and where can you plant new seeds in the
things of God?*

Week 20: *Never Outnumbered*

※

2 Kings 6:16
*And he answered, Fear not:
for they that be with us
are more than they that be with them*

※

An underdog captures the affection of many. The little guy with the big heart inspires us. This is the person who has the courage to stand up against an entity that is much bigger, stronger, is more prestigious or has more expertise than he does. The underdog is up for the challenge, even when the odds are not in his favor.

More (adjective): greater in quantity, amount, or number; a quantifier meaning greater in size or amount or extent or degree

However, in your own life, the underdog plight is not as much fun to live as it is to watch in the life of another.

It can be very intimidating to face a situation where all the odds are stacked against you. Do you remember in your childhood where numbers mattered…how many friends you had, how much money your parents made, how many toys you had, etc.? As an adult, numbers and size still have an impact. There may be times when you must face an opposition that appears to have much more than you. Here are a few examples:

- Standing up for something right and the opposition has more support

- Paying off bills against an increasing interest rate and mound of debt

- Competing for a title and the other team is far greater – larger in numbers and size

- Going through a legal battle and the opposing side has more lawyers and deeper pockets

- Fighting a disease that has taken more lives than has survivors

- Going for an interview or audition and everyone else seems more qualified and experienced

This week's Scripture is straightforward; you have more with God than your adversaries.

There is no need to fear. You have more of everything you need when you are in a crisis. Elisha spoke these words to his servant to calm him after seeing that their enemy had surrounded them on every side. Elisha prayed to God for his servant's spiritual eyes to be opened so that he could see the mighty chariots of God that far outnumbered their enemy's army brigade.

This Scripture is one you can meditate and confess when you experience situations that are overwhelming. It can be very encouraging to your spirit. While you are in the midst of a battle, you can be distracted and have difficulty seeing past it. If you focus on our opponents, they can and will block your view of victory. Just like with Elisha, you may have to pray for your spiritual eyes to be opened. Elisha also prayed what he wanted God to do with his enemies and God did so at his word.

Pray for your victory. Pray that your spiritual eyes will see God's mighty army fighting with, as well as, for you. His army can go into the enemy's camp undetected. It never gets tired. His army is never afraid and it is always greater in size and power than the enemy. Speak favor and dominance over your situation in the midst of praising God.

Maybe you are in agreement with a group of Believers coming together to battle a sizable enemy. It could be an attack on your community, business, school or church by forces of wickedness. There is a Scripture that can encourage you all.

*And five of you shall chase an hundred, and an hundred of you shall put ten thousand to flight: and your enemies shall fall before you by the sword. - **Leviticus 26:8***

No matter what the odds are, even if they are 100 to 1 against you, you still win. You may look like the underdog, but with God you have the most powerful army on your side.

God knows you will come up against much opposition in this world when you decide to live righteously. He equips you with an army that is always ready to conquer the enemy on your behalf. His Word puts you at ease knowing that you are never outnumbered, despite what it looks like in the natural realm. Have faith and trust that God is already on the battlefield.

> Open your spiritual eyes to see that you always have more with the power of God!

Journal Reflections

Read 2 Kings Chapter 6 in its entirety.

Describe a time when you felt like you were up against something larger than you in size and might.

How were you victorious in that situation?

How can you stay focused on God while you feel overwhelmed?

Find a Scripture(s) that makes you feel more powerful and eliminates your fear.

Week 21: *Peace*

ಖಾಡಿ

Isaiah 32:17-18
*And the work of righteousness shall be peace;
and the effect of righteousness quietness and
assurance for ever. And my people shall dwell
in a peaceable habitation, and in sure dwellings,
and in quiet resting places;*

ಖಾಡಿ

There is a beauty surrounding peace that attracts men and women from all walks of life and from every corner of the earth. Peace is associated with a good life, health, freedom and happiness. It is a precious state of being that money cannot buy. There are many ways people try to acquire and sustain peace. Some isolate themselves or leave a hostile situation. Others perform rituals of breathing, chanting or taking drugs. Some try to live a simplistic lifestyle. Unfortunately, there are those who go to the extreme because they are deceived. They take their own life or the life of others to obtain a peace they think comes with the finality of death on earth.

Peace (noun): a state of quiet or tranquility; freedom from disturbance or agitation, fear, terror, anger, anxiety or the like; calmness; quiet of conscience

This week's Scripture explains that peace comes through righteousness - being right with God and accepting Jesus Christ as Savior of the world.

According to the Word of God, true and everlasting peace comes from living a life pleasing to Him as well as, being right with Him.

Righteousness (noun): adhering to moral principles; purity of heart and rectitude of life; conformity of heart and life to the divine law; the perfection or holiness of God's nature

How can you live righteously?

First, you must be right with God. Surrender to Him and accept the free gift of Salvation. Then, begin seeking Him. The Bible defines righteousness as by being born of Jesus Christ and knowing (having a personal relationship with) God.

If ye know that he is righteous, ye know that every one that doeth righteousness is born of him. - **1 John 2:29**

*Even the righteousness of God which is by faith of Jesus Christ
unto all and upon all them that believe:
for there is no difference:* - **Romans 3:22**

With new knowledge and a renewed mind to His principles, your life will naturally reflect the righteousness of God. Knowledge on how to obtain peace through righteousness can change your life. No longer do you have to search for peace, leave situations to find peace, blame others for not bringing peace or force yourself into some self-induced state of relaxation to experience peace. True and everlasting peace does not come that way. You please God by seeking Him, obeying His Word, and living by faith. You will soon experience what some people describe in the midst of horrible situations as - *"a peace came over me."*

Peace is especially desired by those who are tormented by demons. It is also sought after by those who have a life full of calamity and drama. You may have searched for peace in life by other methods rather than pleasing God. Isolation can remove physical distractions temporarily, but your spirit and mental state are not receiving the peace of God. Alcohol and other drugs pacify for the moment, but they create a false sense of relaxation. It only appeases for the moment, but does not bring peace at all. After the effects wear off, the issues of life are still present. Being still and quiet can help with embracing calmness, but it can be difficult to maintain with a busy lifestyle. Some who appear to be calm or peaceful on the outside: soft spoken, laid back personality, slow to anger, seemingly no problems; are not so peaceful on the inside.

They often battle deep-rooted spiritual and emotional issues. No matter how people attempt to create their own peace, their efforts cannot produce an everlasting and all-encompassing peace that God provides.

When you live in righteousness and where the righteous are in rule, the Word of God confirms you will live in safe and secure neighborhoods. It is important to fellowship with and support righteous leadership. As Believers, we do suffer persecution on different levels, but we possess a quiet assurance and trust with God. Peace, security and *"quietness"* will come despite the circumstance around you. Unlike anything else, peace from God covers you with a protection against the issues of the world.

Peace I leave with you, my peace I give unto you: not as the world giveth, give I unto you. Let not your heart be troubled, neither let it be afraid. - **John 14:27**

You can have the perfect peace of God. A perfect peace that covers everything: peace of mind, peace in your home, peace in your body and a beautiful, spiritual peace. He wants you to have His peace and dwell there. Ultimately, peace comes from God, its creator.

Live a life pleasing to God and receive the power of perfect peace! (that's a tongue twister)

Journal Reflections

Read two Chapters this week: Isaiah 32 and John 14.
Describe what gives you peace of mind and security.
Describe a peaceable habitation.
What areas in your life do you desire peace and calmness?
Pray to receive peace in these areas.
List what changes (if any) you would make in your actions, words or thoughts to live a life pleasing to God.

Week 22:
Delivered from the Wicked

ಇನಿಂ

Psalm 97:10
Ye that love the Lord, hate evil:
he preserveth the souls of his saints;
he delivereth them out of the hand of the wicked.

ಇಃಂ

Look at the evening news, local or international. There will be a story, each and every day, of how someone has fallen prey to wickedness. There is no doubt the world is filled with it. Wickedness never ceases. It plots behind closed doors, in secret hideouts and in dark places. Wickedness can be prominent and domineering or subtle and suggestive. Either way, wickedness wants to rule over others and advance its evil agenda.

Evil (noun): having bad qualities of a natural or moral kind; wicked; mischievous; corrupt; perverse; wrong; unfortunate; unhappy; producing sorrow, distress, injury or calamity

Wicked (adjective): evil in principle or practice; deviating from the divine law; addicted to vice; having committed unrighteous acts; cursed; baneful; pernicious; sinful; immoral;

Wickedness has no rules, no limits, no decency and no restraints, but is extremely loyal to its own. There are certain characteristics that warn of a wicked presence among you:

Cruel	Abusive	Vengeful	Greedy
Deceitful	Seductive	Mischievous	Liar
Nastiness	Sneakiness		Fornication
Unscrupulous	Unethical	Corrupt	Vindictive
Sexism	Racism	Hostile	Violent
Manipulative	Overly Charming	Mean	Spiteful
Jealousy	Destructive		Blasphemy

Wickedness can be hard to detect for those who have never before encountered its traits. Children and adolescence are vulnerable to the illusiveness of wickedness. It can be unrelenting and wear its victim down to a point that they also become wicked to avoid further pain. This is one reason why it is so important to pray for our youth. As a parent, guardian, family member or friend, you can pray for their protection.

**You read how God wants you to love in week three.
Now, this week's Scripture tells you that
those who love God - hate evil.**

Hate (verb): to dislike so strong that it demands action; to have a great aversion to; to abhor, detest, and abominate

It is interesting to discover that one definition of hate is *to be very unwilling*. God wants all who love Him to be unwilling to evil. When you detest evil, God protects you and delivers you.

Deliver (verb): to free; to release, as from restraint; to set at liberty; to deliver one from captivity; to rescue or save

God does not want wickedness to have any control over you. Wickedness and evil can work through others who have one or more of the traits mentioned earlier. In some extreme cases, they will continue to cause you anguish until you are delivered through the power of God. I have personally experienced His deliverance. At one point in my life, I was being governed daily by wickedness. I did not realize or detect the evil that was causing my torment in the beginning. I was on an emotional roller coaster and needed help…serious help. When I finally stopped fighting in my own strength and sought divine intervention, the Holy Spirit was able to come in and comfort me. If I had not sought God in that particular situation, the wickedness would have probably killed me.

The Holy Spirit told me to stop willingly practice sin and stop associating with those who portray wickedness. It was now the time to hate evil. This was an extreme challenge. I knew in my heart that some of the things I engaged in were not of God, but I did not know how to break away or stop them. For a simple example, I mingled with married people participating in inappropriate behavior with others when their spouses were not present. No one else seemed to care - it was not my business to say or do anything. I witnessed many other things that made me question what went on when I was not present. My own actions, words and lack of action were not a reflection of the God I loved. I could not figure out why I kept suppressing the uneasiness I felt within my spirit from this ungodly lifestyle. Until that revelation, I was not aware of how much I tolerated and entertained wickedness around me. I finally understood how my own perpetual sin opens the door to wickedness and makes it easier for evil to have place in my life. The time had come for me to repent and make a change.

Abstain from all appearance of evil. **– 1 Thessalonians 5:22**

As you focus on the Word of God and His promises, it becomes easier to be unwilling to evil. Your love for God will grow and suddenly, wickedness will lose its power over you. You will be delivered out of its hands. Praise God!

Freedom from wickedness is a true blessing. All you have to do is love God and be willing to change. God requires you to choose Him so that He can lead and protect you. However, there is a consequence if you do not choose Him and continue to ignore His warnings. He will give you up to yourself and the wickedness you choose to honor instead. This is not a victorious life.

Wherefore God also gave them up to uncleanness through the lusts of their own hearts, to dishonour their own bodies between themselves: Who changed the truth of God into a lie, and worshipped and served the creature more than the Creator, who is blessed for ever. Amen. – **Romans 1:24-25**

God will always, and in all circumstances, deliver you out of bondage when you surrender to Him. You will not have any fear or worry of wickedness having dominion in your life. You will cherish your new life out of bondage. There is so much to be thankful for. If you are new to this process, God helps you along the way.

The LORD preserveth all them that love him: but all the wicked will he destroy. - **Psalm 145:20**

Love God and you will have power over wickedness!

Journal Reflections

Read two Chapters this week: Psalm 97 and Romans 1.

Do you feel that you are in bondage to wickedness?

If so, how have you tried to free yourself?

Why do you believe God can deliver you?

Are there any areas of your life where you are tolerating sin? Explain.

Are there any areas of your life where you are practicing sin and need to repent? Explain.

How do you show your love for God?

Week 23: *Your Fortress*

ಸಿಂಆ

Psalm 71:3
Be thou my strong habitation,
whereunto I may continually resort:
thou hast given commandment to save me;
for thou art my rock and my fortress.

ಸಿಂಆ

"There's no place like home." The character, Dorothy, spoke that famous movie line in the classic Wizard of Oz. Even in a make-believe place, nothing compares to going back home. Home is where loved ones are. Home is where you are safe and your needs are met. A place where you are accepted, encouraged, and loved. Home is where you can rest and relax. For those who travel often and have to leave their family behind for military, business or any other reason, there is still a preference for the warmth of their own home.

Unfortunately, many homes are not like the one described. Some are plagued with stress, division, abuse and turmoil. They have become a place to avoid instead of a place of retreat and tranquility. For some, home is a dark place. Secrets, lies and inappropriate behavior are hidden behind closed doors. It can feel like a prison instead of a place of security and love. When there is no home, mankind looks for it somewhere else. Home is substituted by another person, another place, a chemical substance, gang or cult. Anywhere "warmth" can be found usually becomes the replacement for home.

This week's Scripture is a reminder that God commands to be your strong habitation and fortress.

God and His kingdom is a place you can always call home. And this is not your average home – it is equipped with everything you need. This home has great power and can endure any hardship that would cause others to crumble. The best thing is that you have access to reside there at any time.

Strong (adjective): having strength or power greater that average; vigorous; powerful; forcible; able to withstand attack

Habitation (noun): place of abode; a settled dwelling; home

You may have moments when you need to go to a place of protection from the outside world. Not a vacation spot, but a safe place. A place where no one can harm you and nothing can trouble you. According to this Scripture, God is your strong habitation and your fortress.

> *Fortress (noun): a fortified defensive structure; a fort; a castle; a strong hold; a place of defense, safety or security*

So how do I access my new home?

Praise and prayer welcomes the presence of God into the atmosphere. Daily fellowship with Him is the access point to enter your new home. His spirit covers you and creates a fortress where you can rest, re-group and prepare for the battles ahead. You may need a quiet place to think about a challenging decision. His strong habitation is the place to abide. You may encounter situations that cause you physical or emotional pain. Enter into your sanctuary of peace. There may even be times when you need to clear your heart of issues that you cannot share with anyone else. Go to your refuge in Him.

> *Blessed be the LORD my strength*
> *which teacheth my hands to war, and my fingers to fight:*
> *My goodness, and my fortress; my high tower,*
> *and my deliverer; my shield, and he in whom I trust;*
> *who subdueth my people under me.* **– Psalm 144:1-2**

Having a secure, safe place where no enemy can infiltrate is important during spiritual warfare. You will need an established fortress for protection while you rest, gain wisdom, relax and rejuvenate for the next battle. Life can get crazy, but through prayer, you will be brought back to your strong habitation. It is nice to have a special place all to yourself where you can receive power and spiritual nourishment. With Him, you know that wherever you are and no matter what time of day or night, you can always come home. God is your rock and fortress and He is always with you.

Pray to God for continuous access to your fortress!

Journal Reflections

Read Psalm Chapter 71 in its entirety.
How would you describe your natural home?
What causes you the need to escape or take refuge?
Describe what would be in your fortress.
How would you praise God before entering into the fortress He provides for you?

Week 24: *Loyalty to God*

ಐತ

Romans 8:35-39
*Who shall separate us from the love of Christ?
Shall tribulation, or distress, or persecution, or famine,
or nakedness, or peril or sword?*

*As it is written, For thy sake we are killed all the day long;
we are accounted as sheep for the slaughter.
Nay in all these things we are more than conquerors
through him that loved us.*

*For I am persuaded, that neither death, nor life, nor angles,
nor principalities, nor powers, nor things present,
nor things to come, Nor height, nor depth, nor any other creature,
shall be able to separate us from the love of God,
which is in Christ Jesus our Lord.*

ಐತ

Loyal fans always support their team come rain or shine. They are the ones that have built a lasting bond with the players, coaches and all involved in the whole team experience. Loyal fans travel the distance and remain faithful through all the controversy. There is nothing anyone can say; no matter how negative or factual, that will convince them to waiver in their loyalty.

Loyal (adjective): steadfast in allegiance or duty; faithful; unwavering in devotion

Loyalty is commendable. It does not require any conditions to be met for a person to continue their decision to be loyal. It is truly unconditional. Think about your own loyalties. What are you loyal to…your spouse, your children, your career, your friends, your family, yourself, your country, your God? It can be difficult to determine in the beginning because loyalty is something time reveals.

In this week's Scriptures, Paul poses a serious question about what type of situations could separate you from the love of God through Christ Jesus.

After recounting almost every possiblity, Paul comes to the conclusion that nothing can separate him, nor you, from the unconditional love of God.

Separate: to disunite; to divide or to sever

God's love for you and loyalty to you is everlasting. It can only be severed if *you choose* to reject Him. In other words, there is nothing on the earth or in Heaven that can separate His love for you, except you.

God's love for you is established.

So what could cause *you* to waiver in your love *for* God? Tribulation, distress, persecution, famine, nakedness, death, principalities, loss, gain, worries...the list goes on. Death seems to be a major separator. When a child or a close family member dies, you may get very angry at God. Even a family pet can cause a deep sadness. You might feel that God did not listen to your prayers or that He is punishing you. Darkness will try to convince you to harden your heart instead of thanking Him for the precious time you shared with your loved one. You may be tempted to disconnect yourself from God and no longer hear Him to gain understanding. The love of God and His peace will provide comfort, restoration and hope to cover your situation. Unfortunately, if you choose not to receive it, you remain separated from His power.

Tribulation and hard times are other reasons that try to disconnect you from the love of God. Losing a job, a home or anything of value can attempt to separate you from Him. Anger and frustration can cause you to focus on the loss when God wants you to focus on His restorative power. Past events, old regrets and leftover shame may also try to disconnect you. A hectic work schedule, busy lifestyle and fame can take your time and come between you and God. Some associations and political affiliations can make you apprehensive in expressing your loyalty and love for Him.

There are many things that can potentially separate you from His love if they convince you to stop loving and honoring Him. You will experience challenging situations, but you must be firm in your loyalty to God, just as He is with you.

There was a situation that tried to convince me to separate from the love of God. I call the experience "church hurt." The church I once attended was a growing, thriving place of worship. There were only a few hundred of us, but we were bringing in the community and sharing in the love of God each week. I was involved in the youth activities, marriage ministry and even ushered for a while. I tithed and gave willingly as an active member. Yes, I wanted to do what I could to assist the pastor and the vision for the church. Not only was I giving, I was receiving the Word of God. I grew spiritually and received leadership mentoring. This was the right church for me and I truly enjoyed serving there.

But then, something very ugly happened. The pastor had an affair with the wife of one of the members. Not just any member, the one pastor befriended and became business partners with. When the news surfaced to the general public, the church was devastated! The pastor was asked by church elders to take a break and spend time with his family and rest, but he refused. I believe most of the church would have forgiven him had he apologized and restored order at home. Instead, he used his adulterous, covetousness behavior to teach a lesson on how we all sin and fall short of the glory of God.

Well, you can just imagine how awkward all the members felt. The church divided down many lines...the pastor, the pastor's wife, the lady, the betrayed husband and even the associate pastor who would have filled in. Who were you going to support? No one wanted to pick a side – we were one big family. Consequently, most members left to find another church home. As for me, I completely separated myself from any church and from hearing the Word of God taught after that incident. That was it; I was done with all churches. Sadly, I allowed the poor decisions of others to influence me in the wrong way. This might fall under principalities, powers and depths. From now on, I was going to read the Bible on my own and fellowship with God at home.

Not surprisingly, my "church-at-home" did not work out so well. Worship times became sporadic, if they even happened at all. Reading the Word, but having no comprehension was frustrating. I had no one to ask for guidance. I really needed to hear the Word of God preached by someone with that gifting. Now bitterness was setting in. I was angry at God for letting such a big mess happen and for letting me witness it.

In the end, the betrayed husband disappeared, the pastor and his wife divorced, the members I loved dispersed, and our building was sold to another church. It was said that many couples who once attended, began having marital troubles that led to separation or divorce. Wow, that had to have been some sort of wicked force to disrupt so many lives all at once.

That was a low point in my life because I actually felt disconnected and disunited from God. It was like we were not friends anymore. But the separation wore on me and created an empty space in my heart. I longed for the connection of a church home to worship God and fellowship with other Believers. Close friends and family continually urged me to visit churches to at least begin the process of finding another church home. After many months, I finally decided to attend a Sunday morning service at a church a friend suggested. I was amazed at how the pastor taught the Word of God in a way that I could understand. My life changed that day and my heart healed from the "church hurt." I repented to God for turning my back on Him and being disloyal. He welcomed me back as if it never happened. His mercy and love is enduring. I knew I would never again allow anything, anyone or any circumstance separate me from God and His love.

When I share that story with friends, I am shocked at how many have actually experienced their own version of *"church hurt"* as well. It seems to be a big separator in these times. It pulls people away from worshiping God, praising Him, hearing the Word of God and assembling together in the presence of God. Some of the causes for *"church hurt"* included:

- a group leader taught their own agenda to manipulate others for their own gain

- a church leader condemned others publically for matters shared privately

- an associate minister lied on others to the pastor to discredit them and get them removed

- a pastor or leader took sexual advantage of children being mentored by the church

- a church leader involved with a financial or personal scandal that divided the members

There are other variations, but I think you get the point. In every situation, there is a common thread...an influential person in church leadership allowing wickedness to use them. Principalities of darkness were working through them to divide and separate God's children. Sadly, their evil actions impeded many from growing in the things of God and accessing His power.

You may encounter personal tribulations or witness perilous times in this world. There are many distractions and attractions to occupy your heart and mind. Know that wickedness desires to disconnect you from God and His love. Your steadfast unity with Him connects your power. Always remember you are more than a conqueror in Christ Jesus. You must be fully convinced of your loyalty to God and His loyalty to you. Your faith must not waiver. Others will see your loyalty and be encouraged. Settle it today - nothing will separate you from the love of God or from you loving Him!

Be a loyal fan of God!

Journal Reflections

Read Romans Chapter 8 in its entirety.

What have you experienced that tried to separate you from the love of God?

Presently, are there any circumstances making you feel disconnected from God's love?

How can you re-connect to His love?

How can you firmly establish your loyalty to God?

How do you know that nothing can separate God's love for you?

Week 25: *No Condemnation*

ಸಿಂಲ್ಲ

Romans 8:1-2
*There is therefore now no condemnation
to them which are in Christ Jesus,
who walk not after the flesh, but after the Spirit.
For the law of the Spirit of life in Christ Jesus
hath made me free from the law of sin and death.*

ಸಿಂಲ್ಲ

None of us enjoy when anyone; friends, family members, or enemies, rehash the worst thing we have ever done. Some repeatedly remind you of our past and hold it against you. Even if a mistake was made and apologized for, there are those who will never let you forget. They do not see you for who you are today. This is a form of condemnation that comes from others. The only thing more detrimental to your spiritual growth is condemnation that comes from within. This is self-condemnation and can last a lifetime. Unless you receive God's forgiveness, you will continue to beat yourself up for the errors of the past. It is impossible to move forward in faith in Christ Jesus when under self-condemnation.

> **Condemnation** *(noun): pronouncing as wrong or morally culpable; declaring one guilty; judging to be unfit for use*

Satan likes when you condemn yourself. It makes his job of destroying your future much easier. He can torment you with guilt and regret. He wants you to always remember the most awful iniquity and the biggest mistake you have ever committed. Satan is banking on the fact that if you dwell on it long enough, you will convince yourself to never live above that point. He wants to keep you in bondage to your past. When you condemn yourself, you get weary, confused and begin to doubt God's forgiveness, grace and mercy for you. Your outlook on life and the future begins to dim.

This week's Scripture emphasizes that there is no condemnation for you who are in Christ Jesus.

No condemnation is a gift for those who have accepted God and His son, Jesus. Why does He forgive you for horrible deeds? God is love. He knows you will make mistakes and does not hold it against you. When you make a mistake or purposely commit a sin, there are always consequences – the principle of sowing and reaping takes care of that. But condemnation lingers long after the consequences have ended. Even if you atone for the past, your mind can keep you in guilt and regret. God's love washes you clean of all your sins. He knows condemnation cripples progress and deflates dreams. You are free from the law of sin and death and released from the weight of condemnation. God wants the best for you!

Can I just sin anytime and God will forgive me?

No, you cannot just sin anytime because your salvation would be in question. You may not have truly accepted Jesus Christ as your personal Savior in your heart if you are not seeking God and repeatedly sinning. Some Christians think this Scripture gives them a free pass to sin. They want to accept all the mercy God bestows on them, but disregard their personal walk after the Holy Spirit of Christ Jesus.

> "...them which are in Christ Jesus, who walk not after the flesh, but after the Spirit." – **Romans 8:1**

You should never want to willingly sin if you love God. Walking (or seeking) after the Holy Spirit is vital to living the life He desires for you. You cannot fool God. He knows your heart and He knows your intent. For those who try to find loop holes in His grace and mercy, they will live with condemnation.

> Verily, verily, I say unto you, He that heareth my word, and believeth on him that sent me, hath everlasting life, and shall not come into condemnation; but is passed from death unto life.– **John 5:24**

However, if you are saved, living for God and commit a sin; He will forgive you every time. He fully supports those who walk in the Spirit. When you discuss your faults with God, He gently corrects you and shows you the proper course of action. Your repentance is always accepted. It is very important not to condemn others. You are free to go on with your life and so are they. Living for God opens up your heart to forgiveness. You no longer have to worry or become depressed with every mistake. Your access to God's power requires no condemnation. With Christ Jesus, you receive the power of life without the burden of sin. Living without condemnation is liberating!

Release all condemnation and live free with the Holy Spirit!

Journal Reflections

Re-read Romans Chapter 8 in a different translation other than the King James Bible.

Describe any areas in your life where you may be feeling condemned.

Are you condemning others or holding something against someone?

Are you ready to forgive?

How can you live free from condemnation?

How differently would you live knowing that God forgives anything you do?

Week 26: *Look Ahead*

ಸಿಂಡ

Philippians 3:13-14
*Brethren, I count not myself to have apprehended:
but this one thing I do,
forgetting those things which are behind,
and reaching forth unto those things which are before,
I press toward the mark for the prize of the high calling
of God in Christ Jesus.*

ಸಿಂಡ

There is so much to look forward to! Your future is loaded with fresh opportunities and new possibilities. Yes, you can learn from your past mistakes, but it is the lesson you want to remember, not the actual mistake. The past is over and cannot be changed. Looking ahead without worry or fear can brighten your outlook on life and increase your faith. Every day begins with new mercies, fresh anointing, abundant grace and favor when you walk with God!

If you have lived at least thirty-five years, you probably understand the importance of forgetting the past and moving forward. By this time, past mistakes may have matured into consequences. If you do not make a determined effort to look ahead to God, you could fall victim to the past defining your future life. On the other hand, if your past life was great, you may get stuck feeling *"those were the good ol' days"* and that your future is a downhill road until death.

Our Scripture this week comes from a letter that Paul wrote to followers of Jesus. Paul states that he does not know everything, but he is certain about this…
he forgets what is behind and reaches forth towards
the high calling of God.

Forget: to lose the remembrance of; to let go from the memory

Forgetting is more than blocking something out of your memory or pretending the past did not happen. As we reach forth to new things in Christ, forgetting also means **to lose the power of** and **to cease from doing**. When you forget something, it no longer has the power over you it once had. When you forget something, you stop doing it and you stop it from affecting you. Forgetting is so refreshing! How many more things do you need to forget?

Satan is the accuser of the brethren and does not want you to ever forget any one of the bad, stupid, selfish or sinful things you have done in the past. He wants you to re-play and re-live the worst of you over and over and over again. Satan does not want you to go forward into the new things God has for you. If you keep looking back, you will keep the same feelings of hurt, shame and condemnation. You may even repeat the same actions. No growth, no change and no power will result in your life when you are in bondage to your past. This is why forgetting the past is so important to your spiritual journey ahead. It is never too late to forget!

Paul urges you to stay focused on God so that you can receive all that God has for you. Once you forget your past, you are encouraged to reach forth to the future and press towards God.

Reach: to extend or stretch from a distance

Towards: in the direction to; with regards or respect to

Paul wanted to inspire and encourage others even while he was in prison unjustly. He was not concerned about his past mistakes. He was not bitter against those who lied on him or those who tried to kill him. Paul was excited and focused on his future with God because he had experienced the power, confidence and joy that result from being attuned with Him. He continued to seek God and go towards Him in prayer and righteous living. Paul knew he was a part of God's plan because of his consistent fellowship with his Heavenly Father.

You can experience this power of looking ahead, too. There is comfort and happiness when you look ahead to the things God has for you. If you are busy looking in the past, you will not be able to see your future with Him. Do not look at the past of others, either. Forget everything in the past and release its hold on you. It can be challenging to look forward and stay focused on God, but as you cultivate your relationship with Him, forgetting becomes effortless; pressing towards God becomes second nature. You have to break free from the past to activate the power of your future.

Forget the past. Look ahead towards God!

Journal Reflections
Read Philippians Chapter 3 in its entirety.
What keeps reminding you of something in your past
that you want to forget?
How do you define yourself in character and values?
How do you think God sees you?
What Scriptures can you find that tell you how God sees you?
What do you see in your future with God?
What can you do to stay focused on your future with God?

Week 27: *God's Word*

Isaiah 55:11
*So shall my Word be that goeth forth out of my mouth:
it shall not return unto me void,
but it shall accomplish that which I please,
and it shall prosper in the thing whereto I sent it.*

Think about someone you know, who you trust that the words they speak will come to pass. You respect that person because their words match their actions and ultimately, match their results. There is something to be admired about them - they are a person of their word. They are dependable and accountable. Their words have more power than most.

And then there are those who you cannot believe a word they say. They tell you that they will be somewhere or will do something, but it never happens. Nothing comes to pass from their words. Disappointment is most often the result when they open up their mouth. They are unreliable and irresponsible. Although they use words that everyone has access to, their words are empty.

In this week's Scripture, God confirms that the Words He speaks always accomplish and produce what they are sent to do.

God's Words are not spoken in vain. His Words are not empty or ineffectual. When His Words are released, their purpose will be fulfilled regardless of the circumstance. No man, no demon and no force can stop the power of His Words.

Accomplish: to complete; to finish entirely; to fulfill or to bring to pass

God's Words are more powerful than the most dependable person you will ever know. The reason for this is because His Words create more than their face value. They have the power to bring things to life and make things grow. They can and will do much more than you expect from them.

Prosper: to favor; to render successful; to grow or increase; to thrive

The Bible is full of the Words of God. All things He speaks to you will prosper beyond your imagination. His Word gives you assurance of who you are, provides encouragement through a battle and they forecast what is to come. No matter the situation, the Word of God restores and creates. In dark times, His Word brings hope and deliverance. In desperate times, the powerful Word of God will guide and restore you.

Reading the Bible increases your knowledge of the Word of God. Meditating and confessing Scripture can expand your understanding and build your faith in His Words. Prayer, however, is vital to strengthening your relationship with God and hearing divine Words directly from Him. God wants to speak to you. He has much to share with you - insight that is specific to you and your life. This direct, personal and intimate connection comes through prayer. When you implement a lifestyle of fellowship, you will be led by the Word *of* God (Bible) and the Word *from* God (His voice speaking to you through prayer).

ಐಶ

It is important to know and understand His Words. He is the Creator of all. When you know what your Heavenly Father says, you have more confidence in His power. Your faith blossoms and your wisdom increases. You begin a beautiful transformation and your mind renews to the thoughts of God. Your words emulate the power and purpose of His Words. You learn to speak life over situations. Now your words accomplish what they were intended to do. You live a purposeful life and experience the manifestation of your words because they are aligned with His. You begin to prosper in whatever you say or do - just like your Heavenly

Father. The more you align yourself with God, the more you are able to access His power within you.

Accomplish more with the power of God's Words!

Journal Reflections
Read Isaiah Chapter 55 in its entirety.
How powerful are your words today?
What words are you living by?
What Words of God are you saying and believing each day?
Do you hear God when you pray or any other time?
How can you begin to hear God directly?
Search the Bible and find at least 3 Scriptures that
record what God says.

Week 28: *Pray and Give Thanks*

1 Thessalonians 5:17-18
*Pray without ceasing.
In everything give thanks:
for this is the will of God
in Christ Jesus concerning you.*

Prayer is powerful! There are many accounts of its healing and deliverance power in the world today. Prayer is a direct connection to God and affirms His specific purpose for your life. Prayer is essential for your relationship with Him. The Bible shares the Word *of* God. It gives you a foundation and understanding of the Kingdom of God. Prayer reveals the Word *from* God especially for you. It is your personal communication with your Heavenly Father.

Pray: to ask with earnestness or zeal; to petition; to implore; to ask with reverence, solemnity, adoration and humility; to supplicate

This week's Scripture tells you to never stop praying.

Every day, anytime and in any place is the perfect time to pray. Whatever the situation, God is always ready to hear from you. You need to pray to stay connected to Him. This is why you are commanded to pray. It brings you into the understanding of His will for your life. Prayer reminds you that you are not alone and increases your belief in the Kingdom of God.

When I was first asked to pray out loud in front of a group of people, I was so nervous. I had no idea of what to say. Sure, I prayed at home, just me and God. But now, other people were listening. All I really knew how to do consistently was ask God for help.

Maybe you started out your prayer life in the same way…asking God to do something for you. You ask Him to give you a good night's sleep, wake you up in the morning, and get you through the day. Or maybe you ask God to heal you, bless you, and keep you from evil…things along those lines. Until the day I was asked to pray for others, I only practiced praying for my requests. I want to share other types of prayer that you can incorporate during your discussions with God.

Types and Examples of Prayers

1. **Praise and Adoration**
   "Most gracious God, I give you all the honor and praise today. You are an awesome God!"

2. **Confession**
   "Lord, I repent for taking money that did not belong to me. I will return it."

3. **Intersession**
   "Dear God, I pray for Angels of protection to surround my child and bring the entire brigade safely home from duty."

4. **Petition and Supplications**
   "Heavenly Father, please help me to lose this addiction and be reunited with my family."

5. **Thanksgiving**
   "Oh Lord, my God, I thank you for the morning sun today."

6. **Faith**
   "Dear God, I believe I can do all things through Christ Jesus who strengthens me. I have honored you and receive my promotion now."

The Scripture also says to give thanks in everything.

Thanks: an expression of gratitude; an acknowledgment made to express a sense of favor or kindness received

Well, that day in front of the group, I was hesitant to pray since I might say something incorrect or forget an important salutation or something. I felt silly because I did not have some deep scriptural reference or prophetic insight. Nonetheless, I prayed my first prayer of thanks that day. I did know how to say *thank you* so I just began to thank God for everyone there in the group. I thanked Him for the building we were in, the people who brought us together, our family and friends, and for the opportunity we had to pray and speak to Him. That was about it. Afterwards, I looked around to see the expressions of the others. Everyone appeared normal and the group leader thanked me for leading prayer. My confidence in praying a prayer of thanksgiving was ignited. I began praying more, especially for others. Prayer can be a simple conversation with God about anything. Do not hesitate to pray and simply thank Him - God appreciates your gratitude.

So how do you pray in times of hurt, anger, confusion or resentment?

What happens when you feel God is not listening or when you think He does not care about the pain you are going through? In these times, you must pray in faith. Pray to remind yourself, and point out to God; that you are, and always will be, on the same team. Despite the current circumstances, prayer can lead you out of despair. Reading the Bible and reciting the Word of God helps with this. At first, you may not be able to see the light at the end. However, be confident and know God has the best for you on the other side. Some people pray for others during times like these to divert their mind off their own struggles. Others continue to ask God for help. You can pray a prayer of praise, although it may be more difficult, it is very powerful. Once you pray with praise to God, your entire spirit awakens. Prayer has the ability to diminish problems and change your outlook. Whatever type of prayer you choose, believe what you pray and just pray.

And all things, whatsoever ye shall ask in prayer, believing, ye shall receive. - **Mathew 21:22**

If you are new to praying continually, do not worry at all. Begin to involve God throughout the day with short conversations. Give Him updates or little "tweets" on your status. He loves when you are in constant communication with Him. Praying flows more naturally with consistence. Create your own prayer space and set aside quiet time in your day to hear from Him. You will experience enlightenment, power and revelation through prayer.

Pray and give thanks to God continually!

Journal Reflections

Read 1 Thessalonians Chapter 5 in its entirety.

How often do you pray and talk to God?

What hinders your prayer life? Distractions? Emotions?

What are you appreciative of that you can give God thanks for?

What are the best times of day or night for you to spend time with God? Why?

Week 29: *New Tongues*

ಸಂಲ

Mark 16:17
*And these signs shall follow them that believe;
In my name shall they cast out devils;
they shall speak with new tongues;*

ಸಲ

Speaking in tongues is a highly debated topic in the Christian community. There are varying interpretations of the purpose and power of this beautiful gift. This chapter will not attempt to prove anything or persuade anyone. It will only share a personal viewpoint and testimony of speaking in tongues. However, this book about power would not be complete without addressing the topic of speaking in new tongues.

There are two main reasons mankind is given the gift to speak in new tongues:

1. To communicate and spread the Gospel of Jesus Christ to all nations and to unbelievers (the ability to speak in other languages)

   And they were all filled with the Holy Ghost, and began to speak with other tongues, as the Spirit gave them utterance. - **Acts 2:4**

2. To communicate directly with God from our spirit without our mind influencing our words and thoughts (the ability to speak in a Heavenly language)

   For he that speaketh in an unknown tongue speaketh not unto men, but unto God: for no man understandeth him; howbeit in the spirit he speaketh mysteries.
   - 1 Corinthians 14:2

This week's Scripture is Jesus speaking to the disciples after He arose from the dead.
He says miraculous signs will follow Believers and they will speak in new tongues.

He tells them to share the Good News of the Gospel with every creature; and that those who believe and are baptized, will be saved. (Mark 16: 15-16). In verse 17, Jesus states there will be miraculous signs. Believers will be able to cast out devils in Jesus' name and speak in new tongues. They will be able to handle snakes and drink poison without being hurt by them, as well as, lay hands on the sick and heal them. However, Jesus did not say these signs *must* accompany all Believers or that it is a *requirement* for salvation.

There is a phenomenal amount of power given to Believers by God through Jesus Christ. Not even the disciples, who walked directly with Jesus, were able to manifest all of this power. Their unbelief and hardness of heart hindered their ability to perform all of the miracles with which they were equipped. According to Scripture, the ability to speak in new tongues gives the Believer a way to communicate spirit-filled messages to others and to God.

When I first got saved, I had no teaching or understanding about speaking or praying in tongues. I heard other people speak in tongues at church and on television but was not sure what to think of it. It appeared they were uttering words in a different language during prayer. When I heard people praying in this manner, I did not understand what they were saying, but did notice they rejoiced at the end. I was intrigued and wanted to learn more. I was interested in understanding this extraordinary ability for Believers and desired a deeper relationship with God.

Soon after researching in the Bible about speaking in tongues, our pastor taught a lesson on praying in the Holy Spirit. Speaking in tongues was explained as a language for your spirit to have intimate communication with God. So intimate, this new language is not understood by your own mind and flesh. Times when your mind is racing and your flesh is weak, your spirit can still pray a perfect prayer. In this example, the gift of speaking in other tongues helps you when you do not know what to pray. Since your mind cannot decipher what you are saying, you yield to your spirit and allow it to lead prayer.

I reviewed the lesson and asked God to help me pray in tongues. Once again, I felt silly the first time I tried. I was alone and peaceful. I started praising God and then just began to babble - *"ba da la ma ca do me te,"* is sort of what it sounded like. There was no special feeling or anything, but I remember the babbling morphed into its own unique sound as I continued. A few days later, an answer to a question I had not ever verbalized out loud, came into my spirit. I believe that when I prayed in tongues, my spirit knew what I needed to know before my mind did. It was *very cool*. I thanked God for the answer. I have not yet had the opportunity to speak in tongues to different nations, but I am sure I will have the ability to clearly communicate should the situation arise.

Praying in tongues has kept me close to God. It was a necessity for my deliverance out of darkness. During the low periods in my life, my mind and emotions were too messed up to formulate any thoughts or words for prayer. I was so weak from the emotional and physical turmoil; I could not find the words to speak clearly to God. But, I remembered the lesson on speaking in tongues and surrendered to my spirit to lead prayer. Most of the time I was crying while praying in tongues, but I continued. I knew I needed Heavenly guidance, comfort and strength. Communicating directly with God and the Holy Spirit gave me the wisdom and power to fight back, to heal, to forgive and to move on with my life. There were things revealed to my spirit that in turn, guided my actions. I am confident that this insight only resulted from praying in tongues. This intimacy in prayer showed me how to receive God's restoration quickly. My witness of His power has led others to grow closer to Him. Now I pray in tongues regularly, not just in a time of crisis. I am grateful to be able to get answers, insight, guidance and encouragement from my inner spirit above what my mind can conceive.

> *Likewise the Spirit also helpeth our infirmities:*
> *for we know not what we should pray for as we ought:*
> *but the Spirit itself maketh intercession for us*
> *with groanings which cannot be uttered.* – **Romans 8:26**

You can ask God to show you how to speak in new tongues. I believe that communicating to Him from your spirit is an element to victorious living. You will be able to hear instructions and insight before your mind knows that you need it. This revelation knowledge will set you apart. However, speaking in tongues is not a requirement to be saved. It is also not a prerequisite to receive God's power. For Believers, it is a special ability of communication from

Him if you choose to use it. God loves you so dearly that He will communicate with you in whatever language you speak!

Discover the power of speaking in new tongues!

Journal Reflections

Read Mark Chapter 16 in its entirety.
What do you think Jesus meant by "they shall speak with new tongues?"
Describe a time when you have tried to pray from your spirit.
Why do you think speaking in new tongues is even mentioned in the Bible as a sign of a Believer?
What would you say if you could speak to every nation in the world?

Week 30: *Sound Mind*

ಸಾಧ

2 Timothy 1:7
For God hath not given us the spirit of fear;
but of power, and of love,
and of a sound mind.

ಸಾಧ

What is on your mind? Your mind is like a sponge absorbing all of your experiences and placing them in categories. Your mind is so very precious, as it determines your quality of life by the thoughts you think. Your private memories and your hopes for the future reside there. Whatever you think, you will become.

> **Mind** *(noun): the intellectual or intelligent power in man; the understanding; the power that conceives, judges or reasons*

Often times, dirt and worldly debris seep into your mind. What you listen to, what you look at, and what you give your attention to; create images and strongholds in your mind. If you are not careful, it will get cluttered with ungodly thoughts. Over time, it may base decisions from a worldly perspective instead of from a Godly one. Your mind may influence you to see the glass (your life) half empty instead of half full so to speak. The danger lies in the fact that all this mental trash fuels doubt, anxiety and indecisiveness. You are no longer able to think as clearly as before. Your actions become based on fear, instead of based on your confidence in God's Word.

This week's Scripture is a reminder that God does not give a spirit of fear.

Fear (noun): a painful emotion or passion excited by an expectation of evil, or the apprehension of impending danger; anxiety; dread; terror

Satan uses anything he can to create an atmosphere of fear around you. He wants your mind so that he can control what you see. If he can get darkness into your mind, then darkness is what you will see. Your eyes only reflect what your mind already thinks. The airways, news, television and internet perpetuate fear, lack, sin and carnal thinking. Be careful not to let them be your main source of input feeding your mind. As mentioned before, fear is crippling to your faith. Satan will use it to steal, kill and destroy your peace, happiness and future success. If fear is present in any area of your life, cut out its source today. Fill your mind with the Word of God.

**This Scripture is also a reminder to stir up
and revive the gifts God gave to you:
power, love and soundness of mind.**

*Sound (adjective): founded in truth; strong; correct; solid;
whole; perfect, or not defective; healthy*

You can receive these gifts by growing in the Word of God. He wants your mindset to be healthy and founded in His truth. The Word of God is like a personal trainer for your mind. It challenges and strengthens your current mindset to expand it to a higher level. Your mind is transformed to a level of Kingdom understanding and peace that cannot be obtained through its own abilities or through the world. A strong, competent mind founded on His truths is essential when experiencing a dark time in your life - a bad doctor's report, the end of a relationship, a financial disaster, or any other unexpected event.

Have you ever noticed how people of a sound mind and who trust God, handle life situations in almost the exact opposite way from people who operate in fear? One person will continue praising God and seeking Him in the midst of the tribulation while another person will react emotionally, curse God and turn away from Him. Fear creates extremes and negative emotions. With a sound mind, you already know that the end will be better than it looks right at the moment. There is no need to panic. The spirit of soundness eliminates negative, *what if* scenarios that bombard your mind while you are down. You can see through the clouded imaginations of hard times. Your mind is full of the promises of God. Your actions are courageous steps forward, rather than frantic reactions to fear. You no longer feel like a victim, but a victor. Instead of preparing for the worse, a sound mind keeps you focused on preparing for the best to come.

Confessing this week's Scripture out loud can cause your mind to instantly do an inventory check of its thoughts. Even while living righteously for God, fear and doubt must be routinely swept out. God does not ever want you to be afraid. He does not want you to make any decisions out of fear. He wants your mind to be whole, disciplined, healthy and full of His truth. He wants you to be bold and unashamed of His Word. God wants the very best for you. He gives you power, love and a sound mind to live victoriously!

> *Finally, brethren, whatsoever things are true,*
> *whatsoever things are honest, whatsoever things are just,*
> *whatsoever things are pure, whatsoever things are lovely,*
> *whatsoever things are of good report;*
> *if there be any virtue, and if there be any praise,*
> *think on these things.* – **Philippians 4:8**

Revive your mind with the Word of God!

Journal Reflections

Read 2 Timothy Chapter 1 in its entirety.
Take inventory of your mind. What is it full of?
What needs to be swept out?
From what source do you base most of your decisions –
education, popular opinion, television, internet,
books, God's Word? Why?
Why do you think a sound mind is grouped with
power and love?
What Scriptures help you to revive your mind and
overcome fear?

Week 31:
All Things Work for Your Good

ೞೀಣ

Romans 8:28
And we know that all things work together for good to them that love God, to them who are the called according to his purpose.

ೞಣ

You hear stories of what some call a "twist of fate." At first the situation looks dismal, but all of a sudden, a random event shifts the outcome to an unexpected, positive end. Usually, this occurs without any effort from those involved. Something wonderful happens in the supernatural to bring about a happy ending.

This week's Scripture brings to your attention that when you love God, He makes all things turn out good for you.

As a Believer, you have God working behind the scenes and on your behalf. He has a purpose for you. God gives you unique gifts to fulfill your destiny with Him. Because of this purpose, you can be assured that everything and anything you experience on your journey will work out in your favor.

> ***Purpose*** *(noun): that which a person sets before himself as an object to be reached or accomplished; intention*

Even if you feel like you are in the worst place in your life, God re-arranges things to benefit you in the end. No matter what you do, He knows every detail of your heart, your mind and ultimately, your life. God does this for those who love Him and who are willing to live for Him.

> *"...all things work together for good to them that love God..."*

There was a time I fell victim to identity theft and credit fraud. My once A+ credit had been completely destroyed behind my back. It was so overwhelming, I felt like I was going to have a panic attack. I reported it to the police and other federal agencies, but they could not actually repair my credit or the emotional damage. That was my problem and responsibility. Until that incident, I never knew how controlling credit was over my daily living. My life took on a whole new dimension. With horrible credit, I could not even change my cell phone plan. Most banking institutions close bad credit accounts so I could no longer use my debit card or cash my own paycheck. Creditors were now taking legal action against me.

Initially, I felt trapped with my back against the wall. Since I had never before encountered this challenge, I was not sure what to do or how to begin to claim my life back. However, I did know God and I believed in His power. I knew I could go to Him in prayer and ask for help. He knew who did this and the evil forces behind them. God knew exactly how it all happened and how I was going to get out of this mess. I focused on His instructions to move forward and trusted Him to handle the vengeance and recompense.

*For the arms of the wicked shall be broken:
but the LORD upholdeth the righteous.* - **Psalm 37:17**

I have to tell you again how powerful prayer is. I prayed and things were revealed to me. I wrote letters, spoke to creditors and did not hide. It took almost a year to restore my credit, but during that time, God worked on my behalf. That incident brought good people into my life that I would not have met otherwise and I received abundant favor. The people God delivered into my life helped tremendously during that time and became instrumental with future endeavors. I was also freed from the bondage of credit – good or bad. A credit score no longer defined me or was a determining factor on how I was going to live my life. I learned how to do so many things without credit. Now, I am able to help others with credit restoration, whether or not, they are a victim of identity theft.

Most importantly, my dependence and reliance on God intensified because of that incident. He was with me all the way. I realized how much I needed Him at all times, and in every area of my life. Despite the wickedness that tried to destroy my livelihood, I came out of that tribulation better than I was going in. My financial and business acumen increased. With my situation restored, I felt stronger, more confident and more powerful. God put me right back on the path He purposed for me. He worked all things out for my good!

You do not have to wait on fate or the forces of the universe to redeem you. Even better, you do not have to depend on your own abilities. Any evil that tries to come into your life will have to yield to the power of God working on your behalf. At your weakest point, He is your strength. God wants you to surrender and trust Him while you travel through a storm. As a Believer, you will have personal accounts of how terrible situations turned around because of His intervention. He can revive and bring life back into any dark situation. Each incident becomes a new testimony of how God changed a supposedly negative outcome into a great finale. His power and love is truly awesome!

Love God and all things will work for your good!

Journal Reflections

Re-read Romans Chapter 8 in a different translation other than the King James Bible.

What type of situations make you feel stuck or victimized? Describe what it would look like to come out of those situations better than before.

How would you describe your dependence on God in those situations and in your everyday life?

Week 32: *Confidence*

ಸು☯ಣ

Hebrews 10:35-36
*Cast not away therefore your confidence,
which hath great recompense of reward.
For ye have need of patience, that,
after ye have done the will of God,
ye might receive the promise.*

ಸು☯ಣ

Powerful people exude confidence. They believe in themselves and their abilities to make things happen. This confidence attracts and motivates others. Their words are concise and their actions back it up. They have the uncanny ability to create the world they want to live in. Some describe confidence as the blended result of how you feel about yourself, your attitude, your fearlessness, how steadfast you are in your beliefs and your outlook on life.

This week's Scripture advises you not to throw away your confidence in God and His promises. There is great reward for being patient and keeping your faith strong.

Confidence (noun): trust; reliance; excessive boldness; assurance; freedom from doubt

Your confidence and boldness, through Jesus Christ, intensifies when you live for God. According to His Word, you will receive all of the promises when you live righteously and in His will. You can move forward with no fear. This confidence can be beneficial when you find yourself at a "crossroad" in your life. This is a point where you know your next decision, and corresponding action, will set you on a path you have never been on before. When you consult Him with all matters of life, your confidence will increase. With confidence, you will override any doubt and fear to make the next move. Even if the decision God leads you to make is uncomfortable, unpopular or comes with persecution, judgment and ridicule; you will know that your confidence will be greatly rewarded. It takes patience and faith to endure until the end.

Why does your confidence waiver at times?

There are many things of this world that oppose the promises of God. Satan uses everything in the physical realm to confuse you, create doubt and ultimately, crush your confidence in God. Without it, you will not have the faith or patience to endure the temporary pain tribulation brings. Satan wants to occupy your mind with fear so you will live outside the will of God. Evil tries relentlessly to deceive you, having you to declare your own defeat before you receive your great reward.

I almost threw away my confidence when my little sister encountered a rare brain virus. She laid lifeless in a coma when I arrived at the hospital. I did all I knew to do as a Christian. As soon as I saw her in the intensive care unit, I immediately prayed, laid hands on her and declared her healed in Jesus' name. I boldly confessed she would walk out of Children's Hospital fully restored. My faith was strong and so was my confidence, but she remained in a coma for days. Then the days turned into weeks, with no physical sign of hope. The doctors concluded she would be brain dead for the rest of her life. She would not be able to eat, breathe, walk, talk, or do anything else on her own.

My family and I just could not accept the bad report. We told the doctors we would not end any life support because we believed God has healed her. At that moment, the doctors looked at us with pity and my confidence took a serious blow. The compassionate nurses who took care of her were extremely saddened at this point because they also believed she would not recover. My faith and belief in a miracle of total restoration began to waiver. I began to convince myself that if my little sister went on to Heaven, it was meant to be. I knew she would love it there. But that was not what my faith and confidence initially believed. Evil wanted me to declare defeat before I saw the miracle of healing and restoration. My patience was wearing down and I felt hopeless and empty. Thankfully, in the midst of this tribulation, the Holy Spirit reminded me to keep my confidence and faith strong despite how the situation appeared. He wanted me to cast my cares and worries on God. I meditated on a specific Scripture to build my faith up and stood in agreement with other Believers who were praying for her.

> *But when Jesus heard it, he answered him, saying,*
> *Fear not: believe only,*
> *and she shall be made whole.* – **Luke 8:50**

That encounter in prayer with the Holy Spirit felt as if I took a deep spiritual breath. I inhaled peace and assurance; I exhaled pain, frustration, worry and sorrow. My initial confidence that my sister would be completely restored and walk out of that hospital returned. As soon as I re-established my confidence, her condition greatly improved. The doctors were astonished at her progress. She began breathing, moving and talking on her own. In the end, she did walk out of that hospital, on her own two feet, walking with a joyful smile. On that day, we all were smiling, too. Her miraculous recovery was a great victory for our family. It took much patience to endure until the very end and receive this blessing. God showed us all His power and the power of our confidence in Him. Praise God!

According to the eternal purpose which he purposed in Christ Jesus our Lord: In whom we have boldness and access with confidence by the faith of Him. – **Ephesians 3:11-12**

There may be a situation where you have to take a stand for something righteous when it seems like everyone else is in opposition. You may feel like the only one speaking up or refusing to go along with the crowd. Walking the narrow path few decide to take is not uncommon for a Believer. Standing for God takes boldness and confidence. As you study the Bible, you will discover that many who loved God (Joseph, Moses, David, Paul, Daniel, Shadrach, Meshach, and Abednego) had to stand alone and suffer persecution for their belief in Him. However, because they possessed confidence, unwavering faith and patience to endure, they came out of their tribulation victoriously.

You must practice confidence in God's promises by trusting Him in every area of your life. Your understanding of His abilities will expand and increase your confidence. You do not ever have to be ashamed for loving and serving Him. As you spend more time with Him through prayer, hearing the Gospel and reading the Bible, your confidence will grow into a powerful force. This force brings boldness to change any situation. Your confidence in Him will transform your life and the lives of others around you!

> Be patient - do not throw away
> your confidence in God!

Journal Reflections

Read Hebrews Chapter 10 in its entirety.

Re-read Hebrews Chapter 10 in a different translation other than the King James Bible.

What or who do you have complete, unwavering confidence in?

What does it say about the Law of Moses (Old Covenant) and Jesus' sacrifice (New Covenant)?

How would you describe your confidence and faith in Christ Jesus the Lord?

How is your level of faith and confidence related?

What can you do to increase your confidence in God?

Week 33: *Shine Your Light*

ఐఁౘ

Proverbs 4:18
*But the path of the just is as the shining light,
that shineth more and more unto the perfect day.*

ఐఁౘ

Light and darkness cannot exist in the same space. Light emits positive energy creating a powerful force that uncovers darkness and brightens environments. Emotions such as depression, anger, fear and sorrow disseminate once spiritual light is introduced. Light is like a natural example of revelation that reveals new things that were once hidden.

Light *(noun): that ethereal agent or matter which makes objects perceptible to the sense of seeing; luminous rays; illumination of mind; knowledge; joy; prosperity*

This week's Scripture tells you that the way of the just is like a radiant light, shining brighter and better each day.

Just (adjective): upright, honest; conformed to truth; suitable; proper; of moral excellence

The more you live for God, the more your light shines. You will stand out in this world filled with darkness. Living a life without compromising to darkness can be challenging. Darkness tries to make light appear excessive and out of place. The world will try to tell you that we all have *a dark side*. It glamorizes darkness with mystic powers, seduction, nightlife and secret societies. It wants to convince you to live in darkness so that you will have the pleasures and benefits of the underworld.

There is no debate that Satan can fulfill your selfish desires, but there is a high price *you* will have to pay at the end. Jesus Christ already paid the price for you to have life more abundantly than you can ever imagine. Once you are born again, you are delivered out of darkness and lightened with the glory of the Lord. Darkness no longer prevails. Jesus makes it clear that He is the Light of the world and those who follow Him will have the light of life. (John 8:12)

To open their eyes, and to turn them from darkness to light, and from the power of Satan unto God, that they may receive forgiveness of sins, and inheritance among them which are sanctified by faith that is in me. – Acts **26:18**

It is important to shine your light. Your light has the power to bring others to salvation. Far too many people struggle with sin and iniquities deep within their soul. They have not received the forgiveness and freedom from sin that is available through Jesus Christ. Others are deceived by demonic spirits that torment their minds with dark thoughts and fears. They live without peace, unaware of the power of light that is within them. You are a representative of the Kingdom of God. When others are in your presence, they should notice a distinct difference in your life and see the light of God within you.

You may be hesitant to shine your light because of what others might say or how they will judge you. They may say things like: *"you think you are better than everybody,"* or *"you act like you never do anything wrong"* or *"now you want to act all holy."* Most people will not accept your light at first, especially if they are in bondage to darkness. They may not understand how you (once the biggest sinner of them all) can be delivered. However, if you keep shining your light despite their comments, you will begin to see its power. Darkness will wear them down and eventually, they will want to be free from it. Shining your light will help them to find God. Those same people, who were once your biggest critics, will be the ones who ask you to help them receive salvation through Jesus Christ. Your light will help them to see the love and power of God!

Never be ashamed to shine brightly!

Journal Reflections

Read Proverbs Chapter 4 in its entirety.

Have you experienced a temptation of darkness? Explain.

Have you ever felt out of place because of the light within you? Explain.

Is your light dim?

How can your light shine brighter for God?

Describe a "just" person. Is that you?

Week 34: *Think Big*

The Prayer of Jabez

୫୬୯୫

1 Chronicles 4:10
And Jabez called on the God of Israel, saying, Oh that thou wouldest bless me indeed, and enlarge my coast, and that thine hand might be with me, and that thou wouldest keep me from evil, that it may not grieve me! And God granted him that which he requested.

୫୬୯୫

Great pioneers are those who dare to "think outside the box." They are able to transcend average. Just because something has never been done before, it does not deter their imagination or creativity. They see things others cannot and they do things others think is impossible. Thinking big, beyond boundaries, creates revolutionary results that can impact the masses.

This week's Scripture is known as The Prayer of Jabez. It is widely studied because of the power that is said to come from this simple prayer.

Jabez is noted in the Bible as a just man more honorable than his brothers who said this prayer and God answered. In his prayer, Jabez gives us an example of thinking big.

"...Oh that thou wouldest bless me indeed,"

> **Bless** *(verb): to confer happiness and prosperity upon; to praise; to glorify*

Jabez simply asked God to bless him. He was not specific as to what type of blessing. Jabez just trusted God and knew He would bestow a blessing above and beyond anything than he could ever dream. Sometimes, you limit God with specific blessing requests that you can obtain yourself...a new house, a spouse, a new job, etc. Jabez left the blessing door wide open, to be blessed big and beyond what he could do or think on his own. Do not be afraid to ask God to bless you in a big way. The more you are blessed, the more you can bless others. His favor and power flows through you to those in need around you. He wants to bless you abundantly, beyond what you can mentally conceive or physically achieve.

"...and enlarge my coast,"

Enlarge (verb): to expand; make greater in quantity or dimensions; to extend in limits, breadth or side; to set at liberty

Coast has been translated to mean territory, influence, opportunity, impact, ministry or anything one is responsible for. Jabez wanted to expand in every aspect. Think about how you can be enlarged to touch more lives with God's love. Do not limit yourself to your natural abilities and talents. You may have already reached the end of your coast. As a Believer, you should be operating from His wisdom, strength and abilities, instead of your own. Think big and receive His awesome, supernatural power working through you to accomplish things you would never be able to do own your own. Your good works can be enlarged to touch even more lives. This requires complete trust and reliance on Him. It takes a boldness and confidence to step out of your comfort zone and into new territory for God!

"...and that thine hand might be with me"

Jabez knew that his request required complete dependency on God. He did not want God to ever leave him. Maybe Jabez knew about people who were blessed and enlarged, but then began to take credit for His blessing. You may know of people like that or have experienced it yourself. Those who carried a weight of responsibility and reward that they were never meant to handle on their own. As God blessed them, they convinced themselves that their phenomenal success was due to their own talents and hard work alone. They refused to be dependent on God or His mighty hand. Sadly, failure was the end result. When God enlarges your coast, it is far too big for the natural you. It requires the supernatural you - that is His power working through you. This dependency on Him requires you to surrender your control, pride and emotional reasoning. You will always need big faith and God's strong hand to do Kingdom business.

"...and that thou wouldest keep me from evil, that it may not grieve me!"

Jabez must have foreseen danger ahead or realized that bigger problems usually accompany bigger projects. He wanted to avoid evil instead of asking God for the extra strength to go through it. Temptation is all around and is what causes you to sin. It intensifies when you are making an impact in this world for God. You may be accustomed to asking God to *deliver you out of* temptation and that is fine. Know also that you can ask Him to *keep you from* temptation just as Jabez did. Once you are blessed and enlarged, the new territory may have temptations you have never seen or encountered before in your life. You have no idea of the magnitude of their enticement. Instead of taking the energy to resist these deeper, darker temptations that want to distress you; simply ask God to keep you from them. He wants you to think big and outside of your own needs. He wants to bless you far beyond what your own abilities can do. Jabez spoke a simple prayer that covered many aspects of being enlarged with God.

Think about what it would take to cover all your living expenses, clothing needs, meals, toiletries, gas, etc. Let's say, you are living honorably for the Lord and have enough resources to take care of yourself. But what if you prayed for increase to help others and were blessed one hundred times that amount? Now you have enough to help one hundred strangers, friends or family members take care of all their needs through God's blessing. Others are now blessed because you allowed Him to expand you and lead you.

※※

Let's take another example. You live righteously and have a successful family-owned business with 20 employees. You are a just owner who provides honest wages and great benefits for your employees and their families. You prayed to God for increase and your mind immediately thought of tripling the size to 60 employees, but you did not put a number limit on your request. So what would happen if God enlarged your business to 20,000 employees with one acquisition almost overnight? You cannot even imagine how to begin to run a business of that size, however, God knows how. With Him, your business is now impacting thousands of households! You want and need His hand to be in every aspect of your business. Your success would be an example of big thinking with God. People would want to know more about the God you serve!

The Prayer of Jabez is simple, yet powerful! It can be fun to think big. Refresh yourself with new thoughts of greatness and impact. God is big and ready to show you how mighty He can be in your life. Do not limit Him with your own boundaries. Meditate this Scripture and notice how it will begin to expand your faith in God's supernatural power to enlarge and protect you.

Think big with God!

Journal Reflections
*Search and review The Prayer of Jabez in different translations
other than the King James Bible.
What or who inspires you to think big - outside or above
your own limits?
What do you feel God is calling you to do that you think
is much too big for you?
What temptation or evil do you know that you should avoid?
Describe a blessing that would enlarge you and others around you.
How can you expand your mind to think bigger with God?*

Week 35: *Leave Fools Alone*

Proverbs 13:20
*He that walketh with wise men shall be wise:
but a companion of fools shall be destroyed.*

Powerful people associate with other powerful people. Most often, they have an exclusive circle of friends that share their same beliefs or work ethic. Their environment and influences are taken very seriously to limit distractions and avoid wasting time and money. They understand that the company they keep will directly impact their future.

How is your exclusive circle of friends impacting your future? Some people think that having a variety of friends keeps them balanced. They do not feel it is important or necessary to keep fools out of their inner circle. Maybe it is because fools offer companionship and fun. They have a reputation of being genuinely entertaining and non-judgmental. They play to our emotions and make us laugh, but somehow they manage to influence us into things that are not so good. Fools have a knack for getting us to willingly agree to something unsafe, ungodly or just plain stupid.

Fool (noun): a wicked or depraved person; one who acts contrary to sound wisdom; one who follows his own inclinations, who prefers trifling and temporary pleasures; an idiot

This week's Scripture is clear... you will be destroyed if you hang around fools.

Other biblical translations state that when you have fools for companions, you will get into trouble and your life will fall to pieces. If you are to be wise, you should only associate with the wise.

Wise (adjective): having the power of discerning and judging correctly; or of discriminating between what is true and what is false; discrete and judicious in the use or applications of knowledge; skillful; knowing

Destruction for those who have fools for companions is a hard truth to accept. Associates or friends, who may live on the wild side, seem harmless. But your association with them, over time, is detrimental to your spiritual growth. Relationships with fools are distracting and draining. These types of friends are always in need of something...advice, money, help, etc. However, they never seem to make the right decision once help is provided and usually repeat the same mistakes. If you pay close attention, fools do not really listen, especially not to Believers, and they seem to always have an issue or situation to deal with. Their need for constant attention can keep you from seeking God and living righteously.

Speak not in the ears of a fool: for he will despise the wisdom of thy words. **– Proverbs 23:9**

In contrast, wise friends impart knowledge and counsel. Wise friends are a blessing because they provide accountability and encourage you to go forward in God. The wise do not just tell you what you should do; they will patiently wait until you ask them. When you are in the presence of wise people, you may feel safe and empowered. Their insight provides a new perspective into an issue you may be dealing with. During extreme circumstances, it is the wise who are calm, prepared, and ready for victory. Fellowship with the wise and grow in wisdom. God wants the best for you.

The way of a fool is right in his own eyes: but he that hearkeneth unto counsel is wise. **– Proverbs 12:15**

You will realize, if you have not already, that not everyone wants to live for God. However, those same people like to be among the righteous. They want the dependability, the love, the light, and the power that comes with righteous friends. Unfortunately, they do not want to make Jesus Christ their Lord and cannot walk on the same path you are on. No longer waste your time and energy with those who are not for you, or for God. Move on, and when they are ready to change, they will find you. It can be difficult to let go at first, but you must leave them alone. You can continue to pray for them, but you no longer have to be subject to them. Consequently, fools are not the best for you to have as close companions. And don't worry, fools make new friends rather quickly. If you need wise friends, pray and ask God to bring some in your life. Divine wisdom is fuel for your power.

The fool hath said in his heart, There is no God. Corrupt are they, and have done abominable iniquity: there is none that doeth good. **– Psalm 53:1**

Fellowship with the wise and do not be destroyed with fools!

Journal Reflections
Read Proverbs Chapter 13 in its entirety.
Has there been a time in your life when you had fools as companions? Explain.
Who are the people currently in your life that you need to depart from?
Describe a time when you have been in the presence of wise counsel.
Would you consider yourself a wise friend? Why?
How can you grow in wisdom with God?

Week 36: *Discipline Your Mind*

ಏಐಷ

Romans 8:6-7
For to be carnally minded is death;
but to be spiritually minded is life and peace.
Because the carnal mind is enmity against God:
for it is not subject to the law of God,
neither indeed can be.

ಏಐಷ

Most scientific and spiritual studies conclude that our minds are very powerful. Whatever it believes, it creates corresponding thoughts and concepts to manifest that belief into reality. Our minds are like a control center, shaping our perceptions about the world around us. It is fascinating what one organ can do!

Minds are also very fragile. Minds can be influenced by many things - environments, drugs, trauma, hypnotism, personal experiences, etc. A life lead primarily by emotions (carnal) and negative experiences can be extreme, always reacting to the highs and lows of life.

This week's Scripture warns you that if you are carnally minded, you are an enemy to God.

Carnal (adjective): pertaining to flesh; fleshly; sensual; opposed to spiritual; lustful; of the appetites and passions of the body

Enmity (noun): the quality of being an enemy; the opposite of friendship; ill will; hatred; unfriendly dispositions; malevolence

If you are in opposition to God's ways, you are an enemy and will never obey Him. If you are led by the sinful nature of a carnal mind, it will bring you to death. In contrast, if you are led by the Holy Spirit, you will do things that please God and receive life and peace.

Spiritual (adjective): consisting of spirit; not material; incorporeal; not sensual; not fleshly; pure; holy; pertaining to divine things

Take a personal mind inventory to examine if your subconscious thoughts are leading you inadvertently into disobedience. A carnal mind cannot and does not want to hear from the Holy Spirit. It is very concerned with self; it is ungrateful and is filled with negativity. A carnal mind cannot receive the power of God.

Medical studies link your mental state to health, happiness and quality of life. The Word of God links your mental state to your capacity to receive spiritual blessings and live an abundant, prosperous and victorious life. One thing is for certain, your mind and the thoughts you allow to take root there, will determine how enjoyable, purposeful, successful and powerful your life will be. The following is a comparison of carnal and spiritual thoughts that can help you categorize your mindset:

A **Carnal mind** concerns itself with:	A *Spiritual mind* concerns itself with
information knowledge	*revelation knowledge*
lack and fear of running out	*abundance and overflow*
vanity and self-exaltation	*humility, Christ working through you*
low self-esteem, inadequacy, rejection	*highly favored and heir with Jesus Christ*
sin consciousness and guilt	*grace and redemption*
worry, panic and questionings	*absolute trust in God*
lying, sneakiness and deception	*truth and honesty*

selfishness, materialism and greed	*serving others, giving and sowing*
anger, strife - plotting, revenge and spitefulness	*peace and righteousness- forgiveness*
jealousy, envy, criticism and gossip	*speaking words of life and blessings*
lust and addictions of the flesh	*covenant relationship with God*

And be not conformed to this world: but be ye transformed by the renewing of your mind, that ye may prove what is that good, and acceptable, and perfect, will of God. – **Romans 12:2**

The good news is that your mind can be renewed even if it has spent a lifetime thinking carnally. Prayer, worship and meditation in the Word of God help to renew and regenerate your mind. Attending a Bible-based church and hearing the Word of God preached helps with understanding and applying spiritual principles to your everyday life. Having fellowship with other Believers can build your faith and strengthen your confidence. Living a Spirit-led life is very pleasing to God. It may seem like a daunting task to discipline your mind to think spiritually all the time, but if you remain steadfast, He will bring in fresh thoughts. To be spiritually-minded prepares you for the power God.

Renew your mind with the Holy Spirit each day!

Journal Reflections

Re-read Romans Chapter 8.

What does it mean to you to walk in the Spirit?

What causes you to have carnal thoughts?

Why is a carnal mindset an enemy to God?

What has the Holy Spirit led you to do or say recently?

How can you become more spiritually-minded?

Week 37: *Guard Your Heart*

Proverbs 4:23
Keep thy heart with all diligence;
for out of it are the issues of life.

The information age poses new challenges. With accessibility to news, videos and updates on almost any topic at any time of the day or night, our lives can get consumed with unnecessary data rather quickly. Often times we know too much information about random things that have no relevancy in our lives. Opening our ear and eye gate to celebrity gossip, sport highlights, financial trends, medical theories, or sensationalized news 24/7 is not always in the best interest of our spiritual well-being.

All this data can form opposing thoughts and emotions to God's Word that permeate into your heart almost undetected. Knowledge of any and everything can cause confusion, doubt, and fear which are detrimental to your faith. Information that is not based in truth can re-direct your life on a path God did not intend for you.

This week's Scripture urges you to give careful attention to what goes into your heart. Keep it safe with God because your life depends on it.

Let's look at another translation of this week's Scripture and two definitions:

Guard your heart above all else,
for it determines the course of your life.
– Proverbs 4:23 (NLT)

***Keep** (verb): to hold; to retain in one's power or possession; not to lose or part with; to preserve from falling or from danger; to protect; to guard or sustain; to tend; to have the care of*

***Guard** (verb): to secure against injury, loss or attack; to protect; to defend; to keep in safety; to shelter*

Why is it so critical to keep your heart safe and guarded? The Scripture explains that whatever you hold in your heart will directly impact your life. If pain, jealousy, bitterness, or resentment dwells in your heart, your life will reflect that in some way. Likewise, if joy, love, forgiveness and gratitude are present in your heart, your life will exhibit those traits.

According to His Word, there is a direct correlation to your quality of life and what is permitted into your heart and mind. You should take care to only allow the promises of God to enter through. The information of the world is not always the truth or in your best interest. Although it seems to contain so much "current" information, it will not help you make better decisions for your life. It is full of deception, darkness and indecisiveness. However, being led by the truth of the Holy Spirit, will guide you with wisdom and enlightenment that the world will never know. The truth of God always remains the same from the beginning of time until the end of time. Your life will flourish beyond what you could ever foresee when you allow the Holy Spirit to lead you.

Your heart is another precious and vital organ. It is where your emotions, decisions and beliefs are birthed. Your heart and mind are two main areas Satan wants access to. If he can infiltrate your heart, hidden behind information overload, he will oppress you. He wants your heart to get so heavy with drama, lies and pain, that it will harden and reject the things of God. Satan wants you to trust the world over the Word of God.

> *The heart is deceitful above all things, and desperately wicked: who can know it?* – ***Jeremiah 17:9***

You have to protect your heart because it is vulnerable and becomes loyal to whatever is feeding it. You must make an effort to fill your heart with the Word of God. It can be a true challenge to block information, images and sounds bombarding you from every digital direction. When information about scandals, disease, recession, division, deficiency, terror; and the like, attempt to take root in your heart, cut them off and do not permit them to grow. The Word of God is an excellent shield to filter out all unnecessary data. Make room in your heart for miracles, signs and wonders. Prepare your heart to be good ground for His Word to produce abundant fruit in your life. Allow your heart to heal and then replenish it with the joy, love and peace of God. Ultimately, your heart will be ready to energize new power.

Be diligent to guard your heart!

Journal Reflections

Read Proverbs Chapter 4 in its entirety.
What issues in your heart are taking up too much space?
What are you currently feeding your heart?
What specifically do you need to guard your heart from?
How can you add more of God's Word in your daily routine?

Week 38: *Haters*

ಐಂಬ

John 15:18-19
*If the world hate you,
ye know that it hated me before it hated you.
If ye were of the world, the world would love his own:
but because ye are not of the world,
but I have chosen you out of the world,
therefore the world hateth you.*

ಐಂಬ

The world will always voice a contradiction to Godly principles. It is almost guaranteed that someone will have something negative to say about Jesus. The world does not care to understand Jesus Christ - the Savior of the world - nor His Father, the only Living God. The world wants you to depend solely on the empty promises and self-centered guidance it offers, so it vehemently opposes the things of God. Most often, those who love Jesus Christ will encounter persecution from those in the world who hate Him.

Hate (verb): *to dislike so strong that it demands action; to have a great aversion to; to abhor, detest, and abominate*

In your walk with God, you may come across what is sometimes referred to as *haters*. They are easy to spot because they do not emit love and are always negative towards the good that occurs in the lives of others. They exhibit the emotions that most often accompany hate - jealously, envy, bitterness and cruelty.

Hater (noun): *a person that is never happy for another person's success; rather than be happy, they make a point of exposing a flaw in that person; one who hates*

Satan uses haters as his *accusers of the brethren.* You may find yourself in situations where others will hate you because of your belief in God, Kingdom principles, His love and His power. You may be ridiculed for praying and walking in faith. Haters may belittle you because you are growing in God and do not follow or accept what the world accepts (i.e. popular opinion, the new normal, a godless society). You may even be condemned for trusting God instead of trusting governments and systems of this world. Haters will not only oppose your beliefs, but they will publically expose every sin, every mistake and every imperfection they can find to discredit you.

In this week's Scripture, Jesus is forewarning you that the world will hate you if you live for God, just as it hated Him.

Why does the world hate Jesus? Jesus is love and offers deliverance to all. Satan hates this because Jesus is the Savior of the world and has the power to deliver anyone out of darkness. Satan wants the power to rule over mankind - but he is only a fallen angel. He want to oppress, control and put people in bondage to serve him. He wants to entice souls on earth so he can torture them in hell. Satan uses people to do his evil work. But Jesus wants to free people so they can make their own choice of salvation and serving God. Jesus has come to rescue those under the bondage of wickedness. Jesus is hated because he loves and forgives us all. Ultimately, He wants everyone to live an everlasting life of love and happiness on earth and in Heaven.

In today's society, people hate what they do not understand. Some people have a hard time accepting that any person can receive salvation, regardless of their sin. They may think it is not fair – a child molester, racist, serial killer - can receive the blessing of God if they repent and accept Jesus as Lord. They cannot comprehend the undeserved, overly abundant love that Christ has for them, as well as, for those who have done despicable things.

Far too many people in this world are suffering from the wickedness that has used others to hurt them. They do not realize it was not the person, but evil forces at work to steal, kill and destroy their joy. Consequently, those who are suffering, seek to be healed from a worldly source or from their own self introspection. When they discover that the world and mankind cannot heal them, some become bitter. When they realize that they cannot win against dark forces alone, some become angry and harden their heart against God. Others are ashamed by the wickedness they have encountered and do not want to submit to the love and deliverance freely available to them. Many will hate Jesus until their spiritual eyes are opened and they understand the truth about salvation.

As a Believer, you may encounter those who hate you that do not even know you. There could be haters that you have never met before who target you as an enemy to their cause. Because you are on the Lord's side, you are associated with beliefs and standards that haters rebel against. Jesus experienced this as well.

"If I had not done among them the works which none other man did, they had not had sin: but now have they both seen and hated both me and my Father. But this cometh to pass, that the word might be fulfilled that is written in their law, They hated me without a cause."
– John 15:24-25

The world does not acknowledge God as the final authority. Living a righteous and godly lifestyle is not the norm for the new modern society. It is sometimes portrayed as a *non-inclusive* or *non-tolerant* lifestyle. Wickedness will try to make anything of God look bad, restrictive and unfair. You must fortify your confidence in God and His Word so that you are not in people bondage worrying about what others may think or say about you. Haters are almost like reminders that you are on the right path. They recognize something good in your life with a negative response. They get offended at your chosen lifestyle and take it as a direct insult to their way of life, although it has nothing to do with them. Haters will act uncomfortable around you and no matter what you do or say, they will never accept you. Too much time trying to appease them can drain your spirit and weaken your power. Besides, haters are fools.

❧❦

Jesus knew that you, as a Believer, would encounter haters. He said in John Chapter 16 that our Heavenly Father sent the Holy Spirit to assist you. The Holy Spirit is your Advocate, your Friend, your Comforter and your Guide. Remain in fellowship with the Holy Spirit to bring truth, peace, protection and power when dealing with those who hate you. Remember, you are equipped with power to overcome all opposition.

> Study the life of Jesus to prepare
> for the haters to come!

If you find the godless world is hating you,
remember it got its start hating me.
If you lived on the world's terms,
the world would love you as one of its own.
But since I picked you to live on God's terms
and no longer on the world's terms,
the world is going to hate you.
*– **John 15:18-19 (The Message)***

Journal Reflections

Read John Chapter 15 in its entirety.
Read Psalm 35 to encourage you if you are in the midst of being hated without a cause.
Why do you think the world once embraced Jesus and then hated Him?
How would you handle someone coming against you today because you are a Believer?
Are you happy for others that God has blessed or are you critical of them? Explain.
Who deserves God's love, blessing and forgiveness?
Why does God give it freely to those who choose Him?

Week 39: *Recover Quickly*

※

Psalms 71:20
Thou, which hast shewed me great and sore troubles, shalt quicken me again, and shalt bring me up again from the depths of the earth.

※

You may have heard people in the sports community say, *"The difference between a professional athlete and an amateur is how quickly they recover."* It dawned on me that most who play a sport just for fun or as a hobby, usually take a substantial leave of absence once they are injured. Professionals, on the other hand, may get severely injured in the middle of a game, and come right back by the next game or even sooner. Professionals not only work to elevate their competitive skills, they also improve their ability to recover. They get stronger, faster, healthier and smarter. Some professional athletes can only produce income if they are actively competing in their sport. A full and speedy recovery is very vital in this case. The sooner the professional athlete can resume play, the sooner they can resume their status and income potential.

This week's Scripture expresses how God will quicken you and bring you up out of trouble.

Quicken (verb): give life or energy to; to revive; to accelerate; to refresh by new supplies of comfort or grace

If you are against the ropes, down with only seconds left, or feeling excruciating pain, a great coach has just the right words to change the momentum and lead you to victory. God is much more than a great coach. He has the words you need to encourage your spirit *and* He is your second wind that quickens you during your times of troubles. No matter how low you fall, He brings you up again making you better and stronger each time.

How would you classify your status as a Believer - *Amateur* or *Professional*? If you said *Amateur*, your walk with God is probably part-time, not really serious and not producing any power or results. When you get what you might call "injured," your recovery time is far too long. You may get easily offended or hurt by someone and it takes weeks for you to resume your joy. Even worse, if a fellow Believer hurts you, it may take you months or even years to recover. You spend most of your time in a pit of despair. Unfortunately, you are so focused on your pain; you have no time to help others. Your *Amateur* status does not make you a good candidate for winning souls for the Kingdom of God.

Now, if you said *Professional*, you probably have a solid relationship with God and you are getting stronger, healthier and wiser with each life experience. You fortify yourself in His Word to remain consistent in your faith. A disagreement or a personal disappointment does not keep you down for long and soon you are right back in the game of life. You understand, and are grateful for, God's grace and new mercies each day.

You know that because you are a *Professional*, you actually have more opportunities to get hurt. However, that does not concern you because your fellowship with God has heightened your discernment to avoid some of the pitfalls that once shook you up. You train harder than most with a consistent routine of praise, prayer, and His Word for nourishment. Most people do not understand your commitment, but the results speak for themselves. Your recovery time is much faster than others and you have more time to do your Heavenly Father's business. No one can stop your forward progress with God!

ಬಿ ಆ

In God's league, anyone can become a *Professional*. He does not want anything in this world to keep you down. God will quicken you regardless of your status. If at any time, you find yourself in a dark valley or deep pit, He will bring you out better than before. He does not ever want you to remain broken or shaken up by the evil of this world. God does not want you to sit on the sidelines and not participate in life. It is time to get up from whatever has tried to keep you down at *Amateur* status. Surrender yourself to Him and He will deliver, restore and empower your spirit so that you can get right back in the game. Start your training with God today!

> Quicken yourself through the reviving
> and restoring power of God!

Journal Reflections
Read Psalm Chapter 71 in its entirety.
What life event has caused (or is causing) you
a long recovery?
What do you want God to deliver you from or
restore back to you?
Do you believe God can quicken you immediately if you accept it?
Why or why not?
How can you train to become a "Professional" Believer?
What would your daily routine consist of?
How will you surrender to God so that He can come in
and quicken your spirit?

Week 40: *Comfort and Strength*

ಸಿಂಡ

Psalm 71:21
Thou shalt increase my greatness,
and comfort me on every side.

ಸಿಂಡ

Motivation and inspiration are powerful catalysts. They can move people to do things they never imagined and propel others to do things they have always dreamed. Encouragement and comfort share in that power and are almost always welcomed by the recipient. They are selfless gifts towards others to help them reach their hopes and dreams.

Whatever stage of life you are experiencing; a little encouragement and comfort can be beneficial. Mentors, coaches, best friends, teachers and family are a few of the people who may comfort you. It is invaluable to have the support of loved ones during the ups and downs of life.

Comfort (verb): *to strengthen; to invigorate; to strengthen the mind when depressed or enfeebled; to console; to cheer or enliven*

This week's Scripture is a part of David's praise to God. No matter what life experiences he encounters, God will increase his honor while comforting him in every way and at any time.

God will do the same for you. He will increase you in whatever situation you are in. He will enhance you, while providing strength and comfort during the process.

Increase (verb): to become greater in number, quantity; to grow; to enlarge; to become of more esteem and authority; to advance in value

You may have experienced a time of need when there was no one around to encourage you or you have felt too ashamed and embarrassed to allow anyone to help. You may have pushed friends and loved ones away. It can seem impossible to think positive when you are at your weakest point. This week's Scripture is perfect for any of these occasions. It is a simple reminder that God is always ready to increase you. He is there for you when no one is on your side and when there is no one to talk to. He is also with you when you are alone or when you are surrounded by a mass of people. God will comfort and strengthen you through any and all situations in life.

This Scripture is one I meditate and confess often. Repeating the words aloud and keeping them in my heart, bring a sense of victory and peace. I have shared this scripture with friends in their time of need, and they too, have felt uplifted.

Try this. Close your eyes and take a deep breath while saying...

"God will increase my greatness and comfort me on all sides"

This Scripture is not just for moments when you feel down or discouraged. It is perfect for times in life when you are filled with excitement about reaching a new level with God. You can recite it when you are feeling anxious about a promotion or accepting a new responsibility. You can whisper it to yourself before an important presentation, competition or audition. You can even make it part of your praise as David did.

Not only will God help you, He will restore you better than before. He will address every area in your life that needs comfort and strength including, but not limited to:

- emotions
- finances
- relationships
- health
- performance
- self-esteem
- faith
- leadership
- decision-making

God's comfort is so awesome because it comes with the Holy Spirit. It has His power to preserve and protect you. He knows that you will need encouragement for living righteously in this world. One thing is for certain - you are His Beloved. When you honor God and ask for His help, He is always there for you.

Depend on God's power for comfort and strength!

Journal Reflections
Re-read Psalm Chapter 71 in a different translation
other than the King James Bible.
How do you comfort yourself?
How do you comfort others?
Describe how being comforted affects you.
Describe a current situation where you need
comfort and strength.
Using David's praise as an example, create your own praise
to God that encourages and comforts you.

Week 41: *You Are Chosen*

☙❧

1 Peter 2:9
But ye are a chosen generation, a royal priesthood,
an holy nation, a peculiar people;
that ye should shew forth the praises of him
who hath called you out of darkness into his marvelous light.

☙❧

There are billions of people in this present world. All of us alive today are meant to exist at this appointed time and place. Each of us is unique with our own personality and gifts. Many extraordinary people have found their calling at being uncommon, original and one of a kind.

This week's Scripture is a declaration of how truly special you are to God. You are chosen to show others God's goodness and how He brought you out of darkness.

Chosen *(adjective): preferred above all others*
(noun): an exclusive group of people

You have been chosen for God's mission in this present time. Doesn't it feel great to be chosen for something so awesome? Being chosen is an honor - you are now in a new position in life. As a Believer, you are not of this world, but of a nation and peculiar people who are set apart. The more you fellowship with Him, the more you will understand your precious worth. His marvelous light will shine through you for others to see. You are not a mistake, no matter what anyone tells you. God loves you and thinks highly of you. Regardless of what you have done, He still chooses you.

Ye have not chosen me, but I have chosen you, and ordained you, that ye should go and bring forth fruit, and that your fruit should remain: that whatsoever ye shall ask of the Father in my name, he may give it you. – **John 15:16**

You may have always felt a little different than everyone else. Now you understand why. When you received salvation, you accepted the distinct nature or Spirit of God. You now belong to your Heavenly Father and not the ruler of darkness. You are made new and come from royalty. Jesus Christ has ordained you and provided everything you need for your mission. He did the same for the twelve disciples. While they were on their mission to spread the Gospel, every provision was taken care of.

Royal (adjective): kingly, noble, illustrious

Holy (adjective): hallowed; consecrated or set apart; perfectly just and good; belonging to or associated with a divine power; pure in heart

Peculiar (adjective): unique, characteristic of one only; distinctive or special; markedly different from the usual

A life with God is not an ordinary one. It is a magnificent, fruitful and phenomenal journey. It requires a boldness and confidence that comes with being peculiar. A life with Him reflects obedience, discipline, love, faith and power. It is a self-less life because you live to do the will of your Heavenly Father instead of your own.

Although you are chosen, you must accept the mission. You must trust God and be fearless. You will not act, think or even look like anyone else. Everything in your life will be *"markedly different from the usual."* Trust God and believe His Word above all else. It is up to you to walk with God to discover all the power and privileges you now have. He is good and will always provide the protection and support needed to be successful on your mission. Being chosen and living a life with God is not what you would call an easy one, but it is a rewarding and victorious life - full of His power!

Never be ashamed of being God's chosen one.

Journal Reflections

Read 1 Peter Chapter 2 in its entirety.

How would you describe yourself as someone being chosen, royal, holy and peculiar?

What characteristics made Jesus peculiar?

Describe someone you know who has similar characteristics.

What privileges and responsibilities do you believe come with being chosen?

Why do you think some people would be ashamed to be chosen by God?

What can you do to stay encouraged about being chosen?

Week 42: *Believe God Is All*

ಸಿಂಡ

Hebrews 11:6
But without faith it is impossible to please him:
for he that cometh to God must believe that he is,
and that he is a rewarder of them
that diligently seek him.

ಸಿಂಡ

Uncertain times can cause people to search for something to believe in. They want to find purpose and direction in their lives. Some seek answers as to why things happened in the past. Others seek to find a spiritual definition of who they truly are so they can live in happiness. Whatever the case, there is an ongoing search for understanding and answers about life, the origin of mankind and his purpose.

Believe *(verb): to expect or hope with confidence; to trust; to have a firm persuasion of anything; to accept as true*

The world offers many options on what to believe. It entertains a vast range of beliefs that oppose God and His Son, Jesus Christ. Usually these beliefs evolve from one man's theory on life and creation. However, God wants you to seek and believe in Him so you will continually find the truth about yourself and the Creator of all.

This week's Scripture explains that you must believe God is real in order to please Him. God rewards those who consistently and earnestly seek Him.

If you do not have faith and believe in the Heavenly Father, you will not experience the power that comes from Him. You cannot say you believe in God, while looking to and trusting other sources for daily guidance. The world has a variety of beliefs that oppose the principles of the Kingdom of God:

- ancient mythology
- idols, statues and deities
- sorcery
- metaphysics
- astrology
- mantras
- cults
- voodoo
- humanism, free-thinking
- eastern and western philosophies
- self-consciousness and self-awakening
- science and universe dependency
- Satanic and demonic spirits

There are no substitutions. God must be your only source and authority when it comes to what you trust and believe. It is all or nothing. You must continue to gain deeper insight into God by seeking Him consistently and establishing an intimate relationship with Him.

If you do not believe God is everything, you will open yourself to other influences. You may find yourself seeking other doctrines or beliefs to cover specific areas of your life. You can easily get preoccupied with making things happen on your terms and timetable, instead of patiently waiting on God and the Holy Spirit to lead you. You may become overwhelmed, mixing the Word of God with other beliefs in an effort to find purpose in your life. This can get very frustrating and will cause your faith in God to diminish. Unbelief, lack of faith and fear opens the door to unnecessary issues manifesting in your life that God did not intend for you.

> *Wait on the* L<small>ORD</small>*, and keep his way, and he shall exalt thee to inherit the land: when the wicked are cut off, thou shalt see it. – **Psalm 37:34***

Times of extreme sorrow or extreme joy let you know what is truly in your heart. Deep-rooted beliefs are revealed when unexpected moments in life occur. It is important to know your Heavenly Father *before* you are in a heightened emotional state. You must have faith in Him and that He is over all. It is never too late to establish yourself in His love so that you are confident in His promises. Know that Jesus Christ has already paid the price for you – your salvation, your healing, your joy, your prosperity. If you have no knowledge of your rights as a Believer, Satan will use your ignorance against you. He will come in with doubt through other beliefs to unravel your faith. Satan knows that your faith is your key to accessing God's power. Without faith and belief, you are disconnected to your Heavenly Father.

Do not depend solely on what others to tell you about God. It is hard to believe in God if you have never had an intimate encounter with Him for yourself. He already knows everything about you and He wants you to know as much as you can about Him. God wants you to believe that He is. There is so much to comprehend and appreciate about God that seeking Him will last a lifetime. He has all the answers to every question. You will experience revelations of truths that will bring everlasting peace, joy and power into your life. You must believe that God is the Creator of all and He is the Divine Power over all.

Continue seeking God daily and your faith and belief will grow. You will discover that He is not only concerned about the big things in your life, but he is also concerned with every tiny detail. He wants the very best for you in all things. Believe and trust that He has taken care of all the specific aspects of your life journey. He has blessed you beyond imagination!

Have faith and believe God is over all!

Journal Reflections

Read Hebrews Chapter 11 in its entirety.

What do you truly believe God can do in your life?

Is there any specific area or issue in your life that you need to seek God for the answer? Explain.

Why do you think a Christian would entertain other beliefs that are not of God?

Describe the most recent or the most memorable encounter you have had with God.

How can you strengthen your faith and belief in God's power over all?

Week 43: *You Are Blessed*

ಸಾಂಡ

Deuteronomy 7:13
*And he will love thee, and bless thee, and multiply thee:
he will also bless the fruit of thy womb, and the fruit of thy
land, thy corn, and thy wine, and thine oil,
the increase of thy kine, and the flocks of thy sheep,
in the land which he sware unto thy fathers to give thee.*

ಸಾಂಡ

To be a Believer is to be blessed, not cursed; to have victory, not defeat. According to the Word of God, blessed are those who trust and believe in God. I once heard someone say "an unhappy Christian" should be an oxymoron. Yes, there are moments of grief or sadness, but long term sorrow and depression should not have a place in the hearts of Believers.

> **Bless** *(verb): to confer happiness and prosperity upon;
> to praise; to glorify*

Blessed (adjective): highly favored or fortunate; enjoying spiritual happiness and the favor of God

This week's Scripture shares that God loves you, He will multiply you and desires for you to receive His blessing in every area of your life.

This Scripture is a good one to study, meditate and keep in your heart. In fact, the entire chapter is a great reminder of how strong and deep covenant blessings are for a Believer. When you read this Scripture, replace thee, thy and thine with your name to make it more personal. Say it out loud as if speaking a blessing over yourself. You can also use other people's name to bless them. Try saying it again with a family member's, a friend's, or even your children's name. From the Old Testament into the New Testament, it is clear that God wants you to receive His abundant blessings.

Blessed be the God and Father of our Lord Jesus Christ, who hath blessed us with all spiritual blessings in heavenly places in Christ: **- Ephesians 1:3**

So why don't you feel blessed all the time?

One reason may be caused by having little knowledge of the beautiful promises of God. Ignorance can make you feel hopeless and unworthy. Knowledge and understanding of

His Word opens your heart and mind to receive the abundant blessings of your Heavenly Father. One definition of blessed describes it as *enjoying spiritual happiness*. Reading your owner's manual (the Bible) can bring a peace within your spirit. This peace brings an inner joy and happiness regardless of the circumstances.

Another reason you may not be enjoying spiritual happiness is because there could be a specific area in your life in which you do not fully trust God. Make sure you are not tolerating sin, fear or other beliefs. Be careful not to take matters into your own hands in any area of your life. Anxiety, grief, depression or stress will try to enter into your spirit to deprive you of your happiness. God wants to carry all your cares and worries so that you can enjoy a blessed life. Letting Him take control is a beautiful and peaceful relinquishment. It is an act of total trust in Him. He has access to resources beyond your imagination to handle any and everything. Each time you relinquish your ways to let Him lead you, expect to receive favor and victory. Learn how to receive the blessing of God without getting in the way. The more you fellowship with Him, the more you will trust His ways and His timetable instead of your own.

ಏಞ

An important thing that can hinder blessings is unbelief. You must believe and trust that God has already blessed you. He gave his only Son, Jesus to bear the sins of the entire world.

He has already cleansed you, forgave you, freed you and blessed you! He is not angry with you. You may need reminding that God has continual blessings for you in every area of your life.

Some people think they do not need God's blessings because they are doing quite well own their own. They take full responsibility for their actions. But as mentioned before, carrying the weight of life on your own shoulders can get burdensome. You were not created to do so. Often times, successful people feel empty or depressed and search for spiritual guidance outside the Word of God. Some highly independent people who practice self-help principles have a difficult time simply *receiving* God's blessings. Others do not accept the free gift of salvation and its power through Jesus Christ. Their accomplishments have made them trust and rely on personal efforts to create their happiness. God's love must be received in order for their spirit and soul to be blessed, fulfilled and at peace while they continue to prosper in life.

> *Beloved, I wish above all things that thou mayest prosper and be in health, even as thy soul prospereth.* – **3 John 1:2**

Surrendering every aspect of your life over to God, even after you are saved, is giant step of faith and trust. It is also one of the most powerful decisions you can make as a Believer. Allowing Him full reign to multiply and increase all good things in your life is essential to spiritual happiness. God is a creator and can make anything you need. There is no shortage of His blessings so they will never run out. He has more than enough for everyone so no one can take the blessings that are for you. There is no condemnation in Christ, so no bad deed in your past, present or future will block His blessings. He even wants to bless you when you fall down or make a mistake. Your only hindrance to receive His blessings is your belief and acceptance through faith. He has blessed you because you are His precious child! That is why you are worthy of His blessings!

༺༻

Pray that there will be more examples of blessed Believers for the world to see. You can be another example of a Believer who walks in love, power and strong faith. Others will be drawn to God by your light. You can show the world how to live a blessed and prosperous life – mind, body and spirit!

Cultivating your personal relationship with Him brings a better understanding of His immense love for you. His love is greater than any force in the universe. Intimately knowing God brings a joy, favor and happiness that cannot be crushed by the circumstances of life. It also brings an inner peace that makes life more enjoyable. He wants you to know, without a shadow of a doubt, that you are blessed. God wants you to be happy, healthy and prosperous all the days of your life.

The more you are blessed, the more blessings you can confer to others. The more blessings you confer to others, the more

God gets the glory. You will draw many into the Kingdom when they encounter the blessing of God through you.

Believe that you are blessed and enjoy
spiritual happiness!

Journal Reflections
Read Deuteronomy Chapter 7 in its entirety.
What areas of your life do you see God's blessing?
What areas do you want to experience more of God?
Describe a blessed Believer.
Why should a Believer be blessed?
Why does it please God to bless you?

Week 44: *Consistency*

ಬಿಡಿ

Jeremiah 17:7-8
Blessed is the man that trusteth in the Lord,
and whose hope the Lord is.
For he shall be as a tree planted by the waters,
and that spreadeth out her roots by the river,
and shall not see when heat cometh, but her leaf shall be
green; and shall not be careful in the year of drought,
neither shall cease from yielding fruit.

ಬಿಡಿ

Consistency has a power of its own. It is a fascinating principle that is similar to persistence. It does not mean to do the same thing over and over again and never give up, but it does mean to be the same in any situation. Economic conditions, human emotions and trials of life test the power of consistency. Trials and tribulations are ever changing and unexpected, but with consistency, they can be easily managed.

Consistency (noun): a standing together; a being fixed in union; a harmonious uniformity or agreement among things or parts

Consistent (adjective): the same throughout in structure or composition; not contradictory or opposed

This week's Scripture is a metaphor using a tree to describe a blessed man whose trust in God is consistent.

A blessed person is consistent in their trust in God like a tree planted by the river. The tree spreads her roots far out and deep into the ground. A blessed person knows as much as they can about God and keeps the Word deeply rooted in their heart. The tree does not fear of being damaged by heat, drought or any other extremes in weather. Instead, her leaves remain green. When there is a drought, the tree has no worry because she always produces fruit in the right season. Likewise, a blessed person does not fear when the pressures of life come or worry about changing circumstances. A blessed person knows that the Lord supplies every need and they will always prosper, even in a bad economy. A blessed person is consistent in their faith, trust and belief no matter how the environment fluctuates around them.

Tree (noun): the general name of the largest perennial woody plant having a firm, main trunk and branches forming a distinct elevated crown which terminate in leaves, which in respect of thickness and height grows greater than any other plant.

Without a doubt, being a tree is easier said than done. Maybe you are like a newly planted tree with roots that have not yet sprouted. You are planted in the Word of God, but ready for your roots to grow stronger, spread farther, and extend deeper. There are too many unexpected events that still disrupt your trust and consistency in God. Job loss, broken marriage, inflation, death of a loved one or even a tragic event tries to convince you that God cannot redeem the situation. Despair, worry and doubt stirs up anxiety in your mind. Fear emerges to distract you from your consistent faith in the promises of God. It is times like these when you must emulate the tree and not be moved by the circumstances of life. You hold steadfast to your inner joy. Keep your peace, knowing that God is always working on your behalf.

❧☙

If you desire more consistency in your life, you must seek God daily. Let's look at the analogy comparing daily fellowship with Him to eating. No matter what how much you eat; your body cannot use the food you ate last week to keep you full today. You must eat new food each day to maintain a nourished state. Likewise, you cannot live victoriously today with the Word from last week. It is not enough to sustain you. Each day you need new revelation from the Word of God and from the words He speaks directly into you through prayer. You cannot live victoriously off the Word of God you received as a child or when you accepted salvation. You would be starving for spiritual food. Consistent fellowship with God and the Holy Spirit will ensure you are sufficiently supplied with the power and nourishment you need for daily, victorious living.

And Jesus said unto them, I am the bread of life:
he that cometh to me shall never hunger;
and he that believeth on me shall never thirst. – **John 6:53**

Remaining consistent with God takes perseverance. You must be diligent in seeking Him daily. When times are good, you seek Him. You are not distracted with enjoying the *good life*. When times seem unbearable, you continue to seek Him. You are no longer overwhelmed and are careful not to harden your heart against God. You become more consistent in prayer even when the circumstances of life fluctuate up and down. No longer is your relationship with God occasional, but it becomes a daily experience of His presence in your life. You listen to and believe His voice only. This intimacy will enable you to be still in your own capabilities and allow Him to take over the situation. Your quality of life will greatly improve with consistency. You will begin to emulate the tree and become enduring in your faith. You will have ability to produce *good fruit* no matter what the season. Consistency in God brings peace, stability, blessing and power.

Solidify your consistency with God today!

Journal Reflections

Read Jeremiah Chapter 17 in its entirety.

Are you like a tree planted by the river with deep roots?

What are you consistent in doing, saying or believing?

How would you describe your fellowship with God on a daily basis?

Describe your relationship with God during unexpected circumstances or tragic events.

What new habits do you need to establish for more consistency in your relationship with God?

Week 45: *Free from Bondage*

ೋಲ

Galatians 5:1
*Stand fast therefore in the liberty
wherewith Christ hath made us free,
and be not entangled again with the yoke of bondage*

ೋಲ

Bondage controls its victims through people, substances, experiences and emotions. It is an oppressive condition that governs and rules over others. Most want to break free, but they have lost the strength to resist. Bondage punishes those who oppose it and shatters their hopes and dreams, leaving them in despair. With no hope and no understanding of their power, the oppressed are left subject to the dictates of the specific bondage.

Bondage *(noun): slavery or involuntary servitude; captivity; imprisonment; restraint of a person's liberty by compulsion; the state of being under the control of a person or thing*

This week's Scripture instructs you to stand firm in the freedom Jesus Christ has provided and no longer involve yourself with bondage.

Never again do you have to be enslaved to the old Law of Moses or to any wicked force on this earth. As a Believer, you are set free from that law and now live by the New Covenant of the Spirit through Jesus Christ. Jesus has already paid the price for your complete freedom. God does not want you to be governed by ungodly laws, forces of darkness or man-made "religions" that desire to oppress you. He wants you to remember that you are born again supernaturally and free from any bondage.

Unfortunately, many Believers are still in various forms of bondage today. Some are in bondage to people and need the acceptance and approval of others. People bondage hinders their ability to fellowship with God because they are too busy pleasing others. Intimate or emotional relationships with the wrong people can create unhealthy soul ties that become another form of bondage. This can cause torment and impede progress in their spiritual growth. Some are in bondage to fear. Fear is the opposite of faith so it blocks them from truly believing in God and His promises. Others are in bondage to the past. They cannot move forward because they believe the past is their foundation for the future. They need to re-direct their eyes and heart to focus on Jesus. There are others who are in bondage to sin and selfishness. Whatever their flesh wants to do, they yield to it – addictions, sexual immorality, violence, corruption, etc. God does not want any of His children to remain in bondage and not live victoriously.

> *Now the works of the flesh are manifest, which are these; adultery, fornication, uncleanness, lasciviousness, idolatry, witchcraft, hatred, variance, emulations, wrath, strife, seditions, heresies, envyings, murders, drunkenness, revellings, and such like: of the which I tell you before, as I have also told you in time past, that they which do such things shall not inherit the kingdom of God.*
> **– Galatians 5:19-21**

Are you in bondage to something - a past mistake, an ungodly habit, an abusive relationship, a desire of the flesh, anger, religious traditions, depression, pride, debt, etc.? Do not feel ashamed. Satan targets Believers and uses forms of bondage to attempt to control your life. He does not want you to break free or shine your light to help others. He wants you to relinquish your power through Jesus Christ of restoration and renewal. Satan wants to restrain you from receiving the freedom, power and victory salvation provides.

How do I break free from bondage?

The first thing to do is to receive the powerful anointing through salvation to break the yoke of Satan's oppression. When you accept Jesus, no human, disease, or demonic stronghold has permission to influence you or lead your life.

You are free from mental, physical and emotional chains guiding you like a puppet, constraining you and tossing you around. God never intended for you to fight darkness and principalities all on your own.

> *And they shall fight against thee; but they shall not prevail against thee; for I am with thee, saith the LORD, to deliver thee. - **Jeremiah 1:19***

Focus on God.

Your next action towards maintaining freedom starts with seeking Him and renewing your mind with the Word of God. Fill your mind with fresh thoughts of His promises. Pray for new thoughts of freedom, peace, joy and love. Then allow them to embed your mind to flush out any fear and build your faith. Imagine yourself free, without torment or oppression of any kind. Envision yourself living a fulfilling, victorious, healthy and long life. The more you fellowship with God, the more you understand your freedom rights as His child. You will stand firm in your deliverance. You will no longer be manipulated by bondage.

> *For ye have not received the spirit of bondage again to fear; but ye have received the Spirit of adoption, whereby we cry, Abba, Father. The Spirit itself beareth witness with our spirit, that we are the children of God: - **Romans 8:15-16***

God wants you to fight the good fight of faith and He will instruct you on how to dominate over any darkness trying to enslave you. Do not waiver, do not look back and do not doubt your freedom. In order for you to help free others, you must be free. Knowing and sharing how to break free from bondage can liberate many others who are subject to the same oppression. Helping others to free themselves from bondage is an important aspect of the good works you are empowered to accomplish. No bondage is greater than the redemption of Jesus Christ. Be confident and courageous in your walk with Him. You will enjoy a life of victory and freedom! Praise God!

Live in your freedom through Christ
and the power of God!

Journal Reflections
Read Galatians Chapter 5 in its entirety.
Describe any type of bondage you have encountered.
What or who have you given permission to lead your life?
Describe what being free from bondage means to you.
How can the Word of God free you?
Why does God want you to live being led by the Holy Spirit?

Week 46: *Means of Escape*

ഩഝ

1 Corinthians 10:13
There hath no temptation taken you but such as is common to man: but God is faithful, who will not suffer you to be tempted above that ye are able; but will with the temptation also make a way to escape, that ye may be able to bear it.

ഩഝ

Fighting an enemy would take on a new boldness if there were always a means of escape. There would be no trepidation, regardless of how mighty the enemy appeared to be. Confidence would soar, knowing there was always a rescue mission on its way.

Challenges in our own lives may cause us to feel the need for an escape. At times, it can appear that there is no way out of a situation or that there is nothing we can do to change it. This makes us feel trapped, hopeless and defeated. As circumstances build, suicidal thoughts may emerge to give a false sense of an escape. Satan presents death, but God offers a blessed life as a means of escape.

This week's Scripture explains that evil temptation is to be expected, however, God always creates a way of escape. You will never face a temptation that you cannot handle.

Temptation (noun): something that has the quality to seduce; solicitation of the passions; enticements to evil proceeding from the prospect of pleasure or advantage

God's rescue ensures that evil does not get the best of you. He is never subjected to the conditions of this world. There is no war, economic recession, disease, financial ruin, natural disaster or personal tribulation that you cannot overcome with the power of God.

Escape (noun): to flee from and avoid the danger of; to get out of the way; to shun; to pass without harm; to evade

Mankind is subject to temptations of the flesh; like hidden addictions or dark seductions. Even emotional temptations like bitterness, hate, greed, pride, anger, depression, vengeance and resentment are no match for God's deliverance. No matter what is tempting you, internally or externally, He will rescue you from it. There is nothing that can happen inside of you or to you that you cannot overcome.

These things I have spoken unto you, that in me ye might have peace. In the world ye shall have tribulation: but be of good cheer; I have overcome the world. - **John 16:33**

Tribulation *(noun): severe affliction; distresses of life; vexations*

Satan uses temptations, persecution and tribulations for the purpose of weakening your faith and distracting you from God. He does not want you to unleash the power inside of you. Satan wants to bind and torment you like a prisoner of war. He will use any and everything about you, against you. The world's deception is that you can take care of yourself, all by yourself. When Jesus walked the earth with human flesh, he too, experienced the temptations and tribulations that come against you and every one of us. He needed God's anointing to overcome them. As a Believer, you need the same anointing. God gave His only Son to endure these hardships on your behalf. Because of this, you do not have to suffer or be damaged. You will still encounter them, but you can and will always overcome them.

Consider the three young men who were bound and then thrown into a burning, fiery furnace. They were tempted to disobey God and avoid persecution by worshiping an idol. However, they were punished for refusing to bow down and thrown into a fiery furnace. The fire was so exceedingly hot that the flames burned and killed the king's men who pushed them in. Although the three men fell into the fire, the fire did not burn them at all. It was explained that the fire had no power over them, nor was the stench of smoke on them. (Daniel 3:19-28) God delivered them from a seemingly impossible situation. He made a miraculous way of escape that no man could explain. God will do the same for you.

Consider how one king was manipulated to make a law forbidding the worship of God or anyone else other than himself. Violators of his decree would be brought to punishment by being thrown into a lion's den. It was known that the king's best leader, Daniel, prayed and worshipped God daily. Other leaders, who were very jealous of Daniel, anxiously brought Daniel before the king to be punished. As a result of their plot, Daniel was thrown into a den of starving lions ready to devour him. Miraculously, the lions did not eat him. Daniel said the Lord God closed their mouths and saved him. (Daniel 6:3-24) The power of God superseded man, beast and circumstance. The king was so outraged by the jealous leaders who schemed to harm Daniel; he threw all of them, along with their families, into the lion's den. Once again, God provided a way to escape evil. Important to note: God not only provides a means of escape, but he takes care of those who work in darkness against you.

Seeing it is a righteous thing with God to recompense tribulation to them that trouble you; - **2 Thessalonians 1:6**

In both cases, the three young men and Daniel stayed faithful to God even when facing unjust persecution. They trusted Him instead of giving in to the temptation to worship other gods. God knows the wickedness of Satan and how the world hates those who love Him. He knows that Satan manipulates people, principalities and circumstances of the world to cause harm to His children. He knows of Satan's desires to throw you into some sort of bottomless pit, fiery furnace or den of beasts; any place that you cannot escape on your own. Satan's desire is for you to feel like you are at the end of your rope and relinquish your faith in God. But the good news is that God never leaves you and will always provide a means of escape for you.

I have personally experienced God's supernatural power to deliver me out of tribulation without harm. God even took care of my adversaries. I have heard miraculous testimonies from other Believers of how God made a way of escape out of a seemingly impossible situation. Your eyes may deceive you if you look around at your situation in the natural. Close your natural eyes and tap into your spirit because that is where God placed your "life jacket." Fighting the good fight of faith requires complete spiritual focus on God and His Word. There will be many battles, temptations and tribulations ahead, but you can escape them all!

> Stay focused on God's power to deliver you
> out of any situation!

Journal Reflections

Read 1 Corinthians Chapter 10 in its entirety.

What trials or temptations have you encountered that, at first, seemed impossible to overcome?

How did you overcome them?

What tempts you to disobey God?

How can you better focus on God and His supernatural abilities, instead of your abilities in the natural?

Knowing that you can always endure the temptations and tribulations of life with God, how does that affect your faith?

Week 47: *Sweet Sleep*

ಸಿಂಡ

Proverbs 3:24
When thou liest down, thou shalt not be afraid:
yea, thou shalt lie down, and thy sleep shall be sweet.

ಸಿಂಡ

Sleep is very important to our health, well-being and longevity. As humans, we cannot survive without it. Sleep is vital for normal bodily functions and for the growth and rejuvenation of the immune, nervous, skeletal and muscular systems. However, more than half of the American population do not get enough sleep or suffer from sleep disorders. According to recent medical studies, children, as well as, adults are affected.

> **Sleep** (noun): *a natural and periodic state of rest during which consciousness of the world is suspended; to be still*

Sleep significantly influences the following mental and physical functions:

- immune system
- mood
- breathing
- weight
- concentration
- alertness
- behavior
- mental and physical performance
- decision making
- memory
- reaction time
- social interaction
- accident or injury recovery
- motivation
- coping with change

This week's Scripture is a message of reassurance. It states that when you are with God, you have nothing to fear. And when you lie down, you will have sweet sleep.

Peaceful sleep is invaluable to the quality of life for a Believer. Sufficient rest is needed to fight the good fight of faith each and every day. This news of sweet sleep is music to my ears. I have always cherished a good night's sleep. But somehow in my adulthood, I began to be tormented by nightmares. I always had extremely vivid dreams, in color, and very real to my subconscious, but the nightmares contaminated my once peaceful sleep. After a disturbing dream, I would find myself crying, feeling afraid, or just worn out from an exhausting night. One thing was consistent in all the dreams; there was always something evil trying to viciously hurt me or my family.

I wanted the nightmares to end. I thought the bad dreams were a result of adult-life stresses: job, family, relationships, bills, etc. I tried to understand what caused dreams and how to interpret them in hopes to regulate my nightmares and make them stop. But they were beyond my control and caused fear to creep into my spirit. I started to show signs of sleep deprivation: low energy, weight gain and emotional stress. I felt defenseless against spiritual wickedness that tortured me in my sleep.

It was not until a good friend showed me this week's Scripture and reminded me of how the Holy Spirit is with me even while I am asleep. I began meditating this Scripture combined with other Scriptures on deliverance from darkness. My spirit was strengthened and encouraged. I immersed myself in the Word of God - listening to sermons and praise music throughout the day and before I went to sleep to help soothe my spirit and mind. It was a process, but negative thoughts that surfaced at night were soon overcome by the peace of God. He delivered, restored and protected every part of my body, mind and spirit while I slept, just as I asked Him to do. I still have vivid dreams, but I no longer have nightmares. Thank God!

He shall cover thee with his feathers, and under his wings shalt thou trust: his truth shall be thy shield and buckler. Thou shalt not be afraid for the terror by night; nor for the arrow that flieth by day; Nor for the pestilence that walketh in darkness; nor for the destruction that wasteth at noonday. **– Psalm 91:4-6**

You may desire sweet sleep. Pain, over-exhaustion, fear, anger, chemical imbalance, stress, unforgiveness, guilt and other factors may have caused you to experience inadequate or restless sleep. Whatever has interrupted your sleep, do not be afraid. Focus on God instead of your situation. He can subdue any and all disruptions. He can make your sleep peaceful and refreshing. Stay close to God because He is with you whether you are asleep or awake. You can have an improved quality of sleep right now. Pray for it and believe that it is done!

For God hath not appointed us to wrath, but to obtain salvation by our Lord Jesus Christ, Who died for us, that, whether we wake or sleep, we should live together with him.
– 1 Thessalonians 5:9-10

Sleep well tonight for sweet sleep is a necessity for strength and power!

Journal Reflections

Read Proverbs Chapter 3 in its entirety.
How would you describe your sleep habits?
What interferes with your sweet sleep?
What do you hear or see right before you go to bed?
How can hearing, reading or confessing the Word of God help you to sleep soundly?
Explain how righteous living can influence your sleep.

Week 48: *Abound*

ଈଔ

2 Corinthians 9:8
*And God is able to make all grace abound toward you:
that ye, always having all sufficiency in all things,
may abound to every good work:*

ଈଔ

The earth is rich in resources. Despite reports of shortage, famine, lack and poverty, there are those who enjoy life in the land of plenty. With so many resources in the earth, all its inhabitants should live in abundance. Our lives would take on a whole new dimension if everything we needed was freely available in abundance. We would never worry about running out or rising prices - what a life that would be!

***Abound** (verb): to be copiously supplied; to be abundant or plentiful; to exist or possess in great quantities*

This week's Scripture affirms God's ability and power to bless you with grace, favor and all sufficiency.

It also affirms that you are well supplied in every area of your life and in every good work that you do. Not only do you have more than enough for your household, you also have an abundant supply to share with others as God directs you.

And God is able to make all grace (every favor and earthly blessing) come to you in abundance, so that you may always and under all circumstances and whatever the need be self-sufficient [possessing enough to require no aid or support and furnished in abundance for every good work and charitable donation].
- 2 Corinthians 9:8 (Amplified Translation)

When you meditate on this Scripture, you begin to access resources from the Kingdom of God instead of from the world. Your faith and trust in His ability must remain consistent. You begin to experience what it means to abound despite the world's circumstances. You realize there is no shortage in the Kingdom. Everything is available at any time because God is the Creator and can produce whatever you need. Your faith and belief bring it into your life. Worldly issues such as natural disasters, terrorism, unstable economies, war and pestilence no longer dominate your ability to live carefree and prosperous. God takes care of every responsibility and you will have more than enough to help others. Praise God!

Sufficiency (noun): *qualification for any purpose; competence; adequate substance, power or means; sufficient resources to provide comfort and meet obligations; ability*

Trusting God for sufficiency in all things will not seem reasonable, rational or realistic to those who do not believe in His power. God wants you to accomplish the impossible, something far out of your comfort zone. He is not looking for you to do things you already have the knowledge, strength and skill to do in your own ability. He wants you to reach forth beyond yourself so you will solely rely on Him. You will be sure that it was His abundance and sufficiency working through you.

The good news is that the power to do *every good work* through His grace does not require any qualifications or accreditations from the world. You do not need a degree, experience, funding or a reputation to achieve good success on the path He has created for you. There is no human or institution that can block you or that can validate you in doing work for the Kingdom. What God has called you to do; He also provides *everything* you need, in abundance, for completion. He brings resources and people to you that will help you on your journey. Discover what God has called you to do by seeking Him. His grace will abound towards you and you will access a Heavenly power enabling you to do all things!

> Go beyond your comfort zone and
> abound in the power of God!

Journal Reflections

Read 2 Corinthians Chapter 9 in its entirety.
What person or system are you depending on
to supply your needs?
Explain any areas of your life that you feel God
cannot supply resources for you.
What do you believe God wants to do through you?
What good works do you want to abound in?
How can you use your talents to help others and
promote the Kingdom of God?

Now the God of hope fill you with all joy and peace in believing,
that ye may abound in hope, through the power of the Holy Ghost.
– Romans 15:13

Week 49: *Truth*

ಸಂಲ

2 Corinthians 4:1-2
Therefore seeing we have this ministry,
as we have received mercy, we faint not; but have renounced
the hidden things of dishonesty, not walking in craftiness,
nor handling the Word of God deceitfully;
but by manifestation of the truth commending ourselves
to every man's conscience in the sight of God.

ಸಂಲ

Information from around the globe is readily accessible to those who seek it. There are numerous articles, reports, opinions, video and viewpoints to increase one's knowledge on any subject imaginable. With all this information, you are challenged to decipher between facts and the truth.

Truth is very powerful, especially, the truth of God's Word. Truth will always be revealed and produce proof no matter how much is done to conceal it. It may take a little time, but the truth cannot be disputed. Facts are much different. Facts require some sort of data and can be manipulated. They usually are based on what you can explain or experience.

> **Fact** *(noun): a piece of information about circumstances that exist or events that have occurred; an effect produced or achieved*
>
> **Truth** *(noun): veracity; purity from falsehood; honesty; virtue; exactness; righteousness*

Let's look at an example of truth versus fact. The facts presented to a jury show DNA results and finger prints at the scene of the crime all matching the accused. However, the truth is the lab technicians running the tests were coerced into submitting false documentation to frame the accused and hide the real killer. All the facts find the accused guilty. What appears to be accurate or factual is the furthest from the truth. The accused did not commit the crime. If the jury knew the truth, it would supersede every fact presented.

This week's Scripture explains your responsibility to handle and teach the truth of God's Word.

It is not an easy assignment, but God has given you grace to teach the truth and be an example of the truth to others. Here is another version of this scripture:

God, with his mercy, gave us this work to do, so you don't give up. But you have turned away from secret and shameful ways.

> *You don't use trickery, and you don't change the teaching of God.* ***You teach the truth plainly.*** *This is how you show people who you are. And this is how they can know in their hearts what kind of people you are before God.* – ***2 Corinthians 4:1-2 (ERV)***

Truth is so lucid that it is sometimes hard to accept. When you discover the truth, you have to make a decision. Either you believe it and act accordingly, or you do not believe it and turn from it. Some people know the truth, but strategically mix truth with facts for the sole purpose of misleading and deceiving others. Unfortunately, there are those who know the truth and hide it from others so that its power is concealed.

One of my most challenging times was when I was confronted with the truth about myself and my life. Some of the facts in my life had been falsified and I was prey to deception. However, time revealed the truth. This confrontation was extremely difficult to endure because I had to overcome shame, but it set me free. I urge you to continually seek the truth because it is freedom from the bondage of darkness.

> *And ye shall know the truth, and the truth shall make you free.* – ***John 8:32***

The truth of God's Word can set you free from sin, disease, low self-esteem, shame, frustration, depression, sorrow, regret, sickness, fear and whatever is holding you captive. For example, it can be a fact that no one in medical history has ever lived after contracting XYZ disease, there is no cure in existence, and the doctors have given up treating you. However, the truth is that the anointing of God can cure any disease and heal your body. All the factual information leads to suffering and death, but the truth of God leads to life.

The Word of God never changes. Strengthen yourself daily with the truth of God's Word. All hidden and dark things must be removed to allow the light of truth to flourish. Be ready to accept the truth about yourself and your Heavenly Father. You must know the truth about Jesus and your salvation. Living and teaching the truth requires you to believe and live it for yourself. Continue to align yourself with Kingdom principles and the righteousness of God.

> *We are of God: he that knoweth God heareth us;*
> *he that is not of God heareth not us.*
> *Hereby know we the spirit of truth,*
> *and the spirit of error.* **– 1 John 4:6**

Understand that some people will be offended by hearing the truth. The truth of God does not align with intellect, sense knowledge or carnal thinking. It opposes what the world requires to obtain power, healing and success. When others see the truth of God manifested in your life, they will not be able to deny its power. It is your responsibility to teach the truth and walk in integrity, compassion and confidence. Be bold and share the truth with others, it can free an entire community or an entire nation. Remember, you are chosen and equipped for the mission. The power of truth allows you to do more to improve your life and the lives of others. The truth of God gives you power to conquer all!

Acknowledge the truth and pursue its power!

Journal Reflections
Read 2 Corinthians Chapter 4 in its entirety.
How do you know if someone is telling the truth or a lie?
Describe an experience of hearing the truth of God's Word that was hard to accept.
Has there ever been a fact of your life that had to yield to the truth of God? Explain.
How do you know that the Word of God is the truth?

Week 50:
Use Wisdom, Take Authority

ಐಗ

Luke 9:1-2
*Then he called his twelve disciples together,
and gave them power and authority over devils,
and to cure diseases.
And he sent them to preach the kingdom of God,
and to heal the sick.*

ಐಗ

Wisdom brings enlightenment and insight. Most often, wise people have acquired specific knowledge or extensive experience in a certain area. They are skilled at sharing their perspective with others, while careful not to impose them. Wisdom, used for the good of helping people, has been respected for centuries by many cultures of the world.

Wisdom *(noun): the right use or exercise of knowledge; the choice of laudable ends, and of the best means to accomplish them; accumulated knowledge or enlightenment; discretion*

Wisdom is the principal thing; therefore get wisdom: and with all thy getting get understanding. **– Proverbs 4:7**

When the Bible talks about wisdom, it is talking about the wisdom from God's Word and spiritual matters. This wisdom comes from simply spending quality time with God; reading His Word, praying and living righteously. Authority is an action of wisdom and a close companion to power. True authority requires consistency, responsibility and certainty.

Authority *(noun): the power derived from opinion, respect or esteem; legal power; a right to command or to act; freedom from doubt*

This week's Scripture reveals the time when Jesus sent the twelve disciples out to do God's will with the same power and authority He has given you.

The disciples had been following Jesus and increasing in knowledge of the Kingdom of God. It was now time for them to exercise their wisdom, power and authority to help others. Jesus sent them into towns to preach the Good News of the Gospel and to heal people everywhere - and that is exactly what they did. Some people listened and believed, while others did not. If they came to a town where the people did not accept them or want to hear the Word of God, they just moved on to the next town without strife. Whether or not the Word of God was received, the disciples still carried the power and authority inside of them. Only a lack of faith and belief can hinder it.

> *And they cast out many devils, and anointed with oil many that were sick, and healed them.* - **Mark 6:13**

Jesus Christ gives you the same power and authority in your own life when you accept the free gift of salvation.

> *Verily, verily, I say unto you, He that believeth on me, the works that I do shall he do also; and greater works than these shall he do; because I go unto my Father.* – **John 14:12**

The more you seek God; the more you will understand the love and sacrifice of Jesus Christ. You will begin to grow in confidence with the power and authority that Jesus placed inside of you. As you spend time with your Heavenly Father and the Holy Spirit, you will increase in Kingdom wisdom. This wisdom will guide you on how to use your power and authority to break free from any bondage of demons, disease or discouragement. Godly wisdom will also direct you on how to help others.

> *Happy is the man that findeth wisdom, and the man that getteth understanding* – **Proverbs 3:13**

At first, your authority may seem hard to believe. The twelve disciples, who fellowshipped with Jesus directly, had apprehensions about their authority to heal and help others. Despite questioning their own abilities, the power of God through the anointing was still on them. The Holy Spirit will also lead and guide you on how to administer your anointing of power and authority. Have no worries if you feel overwhelmed or unqualified. Jesus also appointed others, who were not disciples, to heal the sick and cast out demons. God will supply grace for you to do His will - it is His power, not yours.

*After these things the LORD appointed other seventy also, and sent them two and two before his face into every city and place, whither he himself would come. – **Luke 10:1***

And into whatsoever city ye enter, and they receive you, eat such things as are set before you: And heal the sick that are therein, and say unto them, The kingdom of God is come nigh unto you.
*– **Luke 10:8-9***

And the seventy returned again with joy, saying, Lord, even the devils are subject unto us through thy name.
*– **Luke 10:17***

All you must do is have faith in God and believe in His power given to you through Jesus Christ. You may have areas where you need to walk in authority in your own life. Lack, worries, imaginations, strife and sickness should not have dominion over you. You have the power to dominate over darkness at all times. You will begin to exercise your rights and take authority, in the name of Jesus, over any and everything that does not line up with His Word. You may begin speaking with authority and declaring things like:

> *In the name of Jesus, I command the tormenting*
> *spirit of depression to leave me right now!*
>
> *Sickness, you have no place in my body.*
> *My body is the temple of the Holy Ghost.*
> *Leave my body now, in Jesus' name!*
>
> *Lack, you are not of God and I do not receive you.*
> *I am the righteousness of God.*
> *I command the spirit of lack to leave me*
> *and my family now in the name of Jesus!*

There is no apprehension with wisdom, power and authority. Continue to seek God first to increase your confidence in this precious anointing. Trust Him and live fearlessly. Seek His infinite wisdom and develop in your authority. Your spirit will let you know when you are ready to perform miracles for others. It is a great responsibility and honor to do the will of God. Continue to surrender your life to Him so He can work through you. Always remember, God is on the inside of you through His anointing. He is also with you and for you. You have the power to transform lives, starting with your own!

> Use wisdom and take authority over darkness
> through the power of Jesus!

Journal Reflections

Read Luke Chapter 9 in its entirety.

Why do you think Jesus anointed Believers to walk with power and authority?

Why do you think Believers are not living in their authority given by Jesus?

What areas in your life do you need to take authority over?

How can you increase in confidence and wisdom to use your authority through the power of Jesus?

Week 51: *Good Success*

ಸಿಂ

Proverbs 10:22
*The blessing of the LORD, it maketh rich,
and he addeth no sorrow with it.*

ಸಿಂ

Acquiring wealth and fame dishonestly is too common these days. Reports of people deceiving others through fraud, theft and schemes just to make a quick buck are truly disheartening. Stories of people who had everything, and almost overnight, lose it all through some form of self-destruction is awful. They usually are seduced by the lusts of the world and give up their family, honor, and respect for a temporary thrill. It is even more upsetting to hear of Christians who succumb to the greed and wickedness of this world. Regardless of the person, the temptation to have it all, right now, is too enticing for some to resist. Getting rich through evil tactics and without God requires a high price to pay in the end.

This week's Scripture clearly states that it is the blessing of the Lord that makes you rich without sorrow.

Rich (adjective): wealthy; opulent; splendid; costly; valuable; precious; fruitful; abundant; highly endowed with spiritual gifts

Sorrow (noun): the uneasiness or pain of mind which is produced by the loss of any good; an emotion of great sadness

Receiving your wealth from God has no pain or loss associated with it. He is a creator with an abundance of blessings that do not require someone else to decrease in order for you to increase. The process of increasing until you become rich through God's blessing should be a splendid occasion that makes you rejoice with Him. No sadness, grief or regret comes with the wealth He provides. God, in His infinite wisdom, knows how to increase you without decreasing another or taking something away from you. When you allow Him to make you rich, you will be productive, peaceful, fulfilled and happy.

For what is a man profited, if he shall gain the whole world, and lose his own soul? or what shall a man give in exchange for his soul? **– Matthew 16:26**

Riches and wealth are often linked to power. According to the world, the more you master your own mind, the more power you can have to achieve your dreams and obtain riches. Instead of God, you can create your own personal and professional success. This worldly teaching can produce results, but the quality and longevity of its success does not compare to the blessing of God. It is limited to the boundary of one's own personal abilities and by the world's resources. Riches without God will lead to self-destruction. More importantly, when the storms of life come, all "man-made" possessions will crumble and whatever is from God will remain.

Lo, this is the man that made not God his strength;
but trusted in the abundance of his riches,
and strengthened himself in his wickedness. **– Psalm 52:7**

As the partridge sitteth on eggs, and hatcheth them not;
so he that getteth riches, and not by right,
shall leave them in the midst of his days,
and at his end shall be a fool. **– Jeremiah 17:11**

When riches and power are gained by self-efforts, one begins to crown oneself God. A person takes credit for their success through talent, intellect, looks or charm. No longer is there a dependence on God - this is where the danger lies. Integrity and patience break down, and reliance on God wanes. A person can become obsessed with monitoring all their possessions and fall into bondage to them. Instead of having wealth - wealth has them. God does not want you to be in bondage to anything. He wants you to receive your wealth and increase without worry or care. He wants to increase you and make you great so that you can be an example for the Kingdom of God.

> *Both riches and honour come of thee, and thou reignest over all;*
> *and in thine hand is power and might;*
> *and in thine hand it is to make great,*
> *and to give strength unto all.*
> *— 1 Chronicles 29:12*

God wants you to experience the full pleasure of a blessed life. He acquires and maintains your wealth for your security. He does not want you to be in fear that someone or something will take it from you. When you yield your aspirations to His purpose for your life; increase comes sooner than expected. Your riches will be in such abundance, you will gladly share it with the less fortunate as God directs you. With Him, your riches will be everlasting!

> *Every man also to whom God hath given riches and wealth,*
> *and hath given him power to eat thereof,*
> *and to take his portion, and to rejoice in his labour;*
> *this is the gift of God. — Ecclesiastes 5:19*

You can be sure that when God makes you rich, He protects your blessings and the fruit of them to ensure your enjoyment. Evil and wickedness will not partake in your riches. Your wealth will not require you to toil day and night. You will have energy and excitement over what God has done for you. Nothing will be damaged from your prosperity...not your family, not your health, not your joy, not a thing. You will enjoy *good success* when He is your source!

One of God's best attributes is that He knows you better than you know yourself. He knows your deepest desires, your strengths, your weaknesses and your individual personality. He made you unique and can work with any skill already existing inside of you. God knows you, so get to know Him and yield to His ways. Seek Him in prayer and He will direct your path to *good success.*

Receive sustainable riches and good success
from the blessing of God!

Journal Reflections

Read Proverbs Chapter 10 in its entirety.
Describe what good success means to you.
Have you ever been tempted to gain riches in a deceitful manner? Explain.
Are you happier with more riches in your household?
Why do you think God wants to make you rich and have good success?
If God made you a multi-millionaire today, could He trust you to be a good steward over the money?
Would you give to others who God assigns?
What would be the very first thing you would do?

> Praise ye the LORD. Blessed is the man that feareth the LORD,
> that delighteth greatly in his commandments.
> His seed shall be mighty upon earth:
> the generation of the upright shall be blessed.
> Wealth and riches shall be in his house:
> and his righteousness endureth for ever.
> **– Psalm 112:1-3**

Week 52: *Victory!*

ಸಿಂಚ

1 John 5:4-5
For whatsoever is born of God overcometh the world: and this is the victory that overcometh the world, even our faith. Who is he that overcometh the world, but he that believeth that Jesus is the Son of God?

ಸಿಂಚ

It is time for you, as a Believer, to win in life. When the enemy of sickness and disease comes to battle, you are victorious. In any competition for promotion or increase, you are the winner. In the midst of a relationship crisis, you have dominion over strife and discord. No matter the circumstance, you always win!

Victory *(noun): the defeat of an enemy in battle; the advantage or superiority gained over spiritual enemies; a successful ending of a struggle or contest; conquest*

**This week's Scripture is an ultimate decree
of your power through God.
For you who live by faith and believe
that Jesus is the Son of God,
you are victorious over the world!**

You win against the enemy of darkness. As a child of God, you defeat all evil in this world. Let's look at two other translations of the same verses. No matter which translation of the Bible is used, your victory is evident.

*For whatever is born of God is victorious over the world;
and this is the victory that conquers the world, even our faith.
Who is it that is victorious over [that conquers] the world but he
who believes that Jesus is the Son of God [who adheres to, trusts in,
and relies on that fact]?* **(AMP)**

ೞఴ

*For every child of God defeats this evil world,
and you achieve this victory through our faith.
And who can win this battle against the world?
Only those who believe that Jesus is the Son of God.* **(NLT)**

Victory with God is special. This victory does not make you cocky, haughty, arrogant or rude because all honor is given to Him for the victory. You are humble, not prideful. You are gracious, not mean. Your victory encourages others and they can share in the celebration. However, this victory requires an element of boldness and submission to God. Every area of your life is subject to the authority of God within you. Whether it is a person, an emotion, a circumstance, a generational curse, an entity or something not mentioned; nothing can defeat you. The world may hate you because you love Jesus, but anything and everything that comes against you will be conquered. You must speak victory out of your mouth like a weapon.

> *"I am more than a conqueror through Christ Jesus and no person or circumstance can stop me"*
>
> *"My life is full of joy and I command peace in my home"*
>
> *"I forgive and go forward in my successful future with God"*

You may think you are not victorious because your life does not appear to be what you desire. Many Believers encounter that same feeling and sometimes become hopeless. In order to overcome this feeling, you must remember to look at your situation through the eyes of God and not through your own eyes or understanding. Victory will not always come at the time you think it should, but keep your faith, it *will* come. Living with the power of God does not mean evil will never attack - you will always have to fight the good fight of faith. Living with God's power means you will *always* win over the sin and darkness of this world! Victory through Jesus Christ overcomes sin and glorifies God.

> *The sting of death is sin; and the strength of sin is the law. But thanks be to God, which giveth us the victory through our Lord Jesus Christ.* **– 1 Corinthians 15: 56-57**

Living a victorious life with God is truly a blessing. Victory is attainable when you trust Him and spend quality time with Him every day. God sent the Holy Spirit to comfort and guide you through each battle. The more you experience victory in your personal life, the stronger your confidence becomes. This will prepare you for even greater battles ahead and enable you to help in God's army. Those who are suffering, depressed and living defeated lives can obtain encouragement from you. Soon, they will desire to seek more about your God and His power. It is important to know that you play a vital part in the ultimate victory - winning souls for Jesus Christ!

Live in the victory and power Jesus
has attained for you!

Journal Reflections
Read 1 John Chapter 5 in its entirety.
Do you believe you are a child of God and joint heirs with
Jesus Christ, His Son? Explain.
What do you want to have victory over? Seek God's Word in
Scripture concerning this area.
Describe victorious living. Does it align with God's Word?
What could hinder your victory in every area of life?
How can you encourage others to grow and live
victoriously with God?

POWER Conclusion

I pray that this book has blessed and empowered you with the Word of God. It was written out of love and a desire to encourage you along your journey to seek God and His power over all. These fifty-two weeks of Scripture and insight were meant to transform your thinking and ultimately, your life. You can always refer back to any week for inspiration and reflection. Remember, the world cannot offer you the all-encompassing power that already exists inside of you as a Believer of Jesus Christ.

Knowing God and accepting Jesus as the Savior of the world is the first step to accessing this power. If you have not taken the first step and would like to, you must believe in your heart that God loves you and gave His Son, Jesus to redeem you of all sin. You must be ready to give your life to God and receive Jesus Christ as your personal Savior. This gift of salvation and eternal life is free! All you have to do is accept it.

*And it shall come to pass, that whosoever shall call on the name of the Lord shall be saved. – **Acts 2:21***

When you are ready, confess this Prayer of Salvation out loud.

Dear Heavenly Father, I come to you just as I am.
Thank you God for loving me so much that
you sent your only Son to save me.
I repent of my sins. I believe and accept Jesus Christ
as my Lord and Savior.
I believe that Jesus was crucified on the cross and that
His blood cleanses me of all my sins.
I believe in my heart that you, God, raised Jesus from the dead
and He now sits at your right hand in Heaven.
You have sent the Holy Spirit to guide me.
It is by your mercy, love and grace that I receive
this free gift by faith.
I am now your child, Almighty God, and
joint-heirs with Jesus Christ. Amen

Record this day as the most important day of your life! You have started the process of complete transformation. Now that your spirit is one with God, continually seek Him and understanding of His Word. You will be a part of the amazing miracles, signs and wonders that come through the power of God!

Please share the Good News of the Gospel with others! I love you and leave you with these words…

Finally, my brethren, be strong in the Lord,
and in the power of his might. **– Ephesians 6:10**

About The Author

AKILAH GRANT is co-founder of Inlite Media and has received the highest distinct honor as Joseph Scholar from The Joseph Business School at Living Word Christian Center in Forest Park, Illinois. She is also a cum laude graduate of North Carolina A&T State University earning a Bachelor of Science in chemical engineering.

Mrs. Grant is an inspirational author and entrepreneur. Her passion is to encourage others to live healthy, strong and victorious lives. Through God's love and power, she overcame pain, anger, betrayal and hopelessness. She now equips readers with spiritual truths to strengthen their faith and improve their quality of life. In addition to her love of travel and the arts, Akilah enjoys laughing with her husband, children, close family and friends.

We would love your feedback!

Discover the companion journal from Akilah Grant,
Power Over All: Journal Reflections and Bible Study Guide.

For more information, please visit www.AkilahGrant.com
or email: akilah@inlitemedia.com

One God and Father of all, who is above all,
and through all, and in you all. – **Ephesians 4:6**

Made in the USA
Charleston, SC
13 January 2013